LIGHTHOUSES

LIGHTHOUSES

written and illustrated by

ARTHUR SMITH

1971

HOUGHTON MIFFLIN COMPANY BOSTON

To the men and women of the lighthouse service
who kept the beacons burning brightly and their
successors in the Coast Guard who so gloriously
carry on the traditions of the "wickies"

Table of Contents

INTRODUCTION

IF YOU HAVE ever been to the seashore you must have visited or seen a lighthouse, for it is as much a part of the scene as the sand and water, the rocks and shells, or the sea gulls wheeling and dipping overhead. It makes a pretty picture on a balmy summer day with the water sparkling in the sun and the blue sky over all.

But there is another side to the picture, a darker, thrilling, sometimes tragic, but always exciting one. In the darkness of the night or when fog or storm blacks out all sight of sand or water, a beacon's flashing light or hoarse cry of warning can spell the difference between life or death for the crew of a vessel that has lost its way.

This is the story of the lighthouse, beginning in the days when bonfires on rocky headlands shed their wavering light on the sea and a cannon's boom echoed through the murk to warn the fog-bound mariner, and bringing us up to the present time when the great lights flash their powerful beams twenty miles or more, and radio waves reach out for hundreds of miles to protect the voyager and show him the way. It is a tale worth telling, a tale of storm and shipwreck, death and destruction, thievery and violence. But a tale, also, of the courage, unselfishness, devotion to duty, and heroism of the devoted men and women who keep the beacons burning brightly.

THE ANCIENT BEACONS

IT ALL STARTS thousands of years before the birth of Christ, with the Egyptians and Phoenicians who lived in the lands bordering the eastern end of the Mediterranean Sea. The Egyptians were probably the first to set up lights as guides for navigation, for the mighty Nile River, five thousand miles long, winding and full of shoals and sand banks, runs like a Main Street through their country. The Egyptians, constantly traveling up and down its great length, erected beacons along the banks to light the way.

On the other hand, the Phoenicians, who lived to the east and just north of the kingdom of the Jews, were deep water navigators who sailed from one end of the inland sea to the other and even out through the Pillars of Hercules. They skirted the coasts of Spain, France, and the British Isles, setting up trading posts wherever they found suitable harbors and people to buy their merchandise: luxurious fabrics, beautiful dyes, and the many wonderful things they made of gold, silver, and ivory. Before long, the coasts were dotted with these trading towns and the lights the Phoenicians put up in order to safeguard their ships and the valuable cargoes they carried.

Most of these early Egyptian and Phoenician warning lights were just bonfires or simple arrangements of buckets or braziers containing burning matter mounted on long poles stuck in the

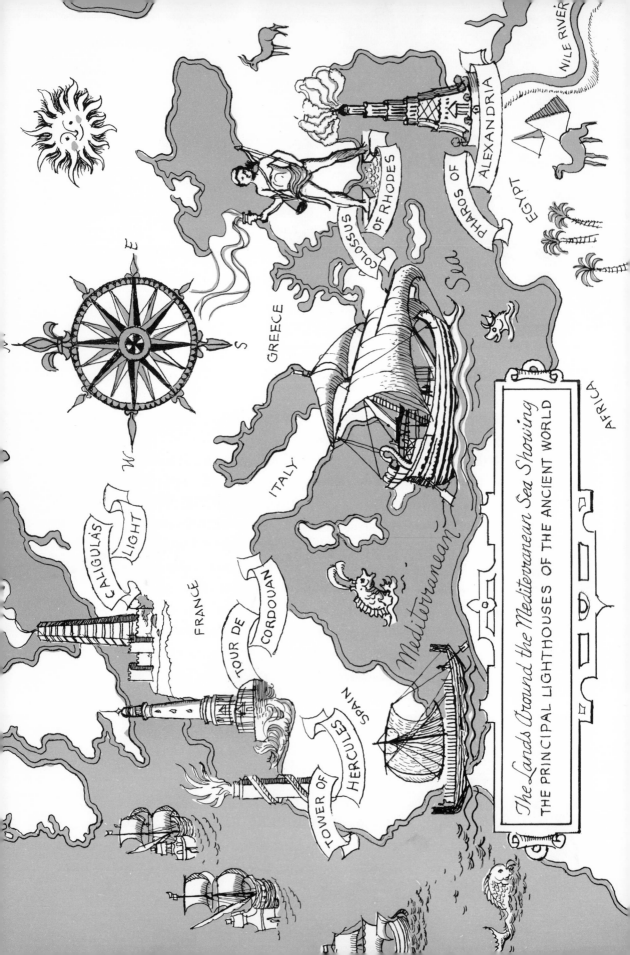

The Lands Around the Mediterranean Sea Showing
THE PRINCIPAL LIGHTHOUSES OF THE ANCIENT WORLD

ground. Consequently, when the Egyptians built a lighthouse in the harbor of Alexandria at the mouth of the Nile, they astounded the world by erecting one of the greatest structures anyone had ever seen. It was the towering and magnificent Pharos of Alexandria, the first real lighthouse, which has long been considered one of the seven wonders of the ancient world.

The Pharos of Alexandria

Three thousand years ago the Greek poet Homer spoke of "lighted beacons for the guidance of the mariner." Later, around 600 B.C., another poet named Lesches referred to a lighthouse on the bank of the Hellespont, the body of water separating Greece from Turkey. But the Pharos of Alexandria is the first lighthouse that we really know anything about.

When Ptolemy II was king of Egypt, he commissioned the architect Sostratus to design a beacon which "shall serve every man who voyages in a boat." The site chosen was the isle of Pharos in the Bay of Alexandria. This little island was connected to the mainland by a causeway, which was a great help, for it made it a fairly simple matter to get men and materials to the construction site. The Egyptians had no electrically operated machinery, no steam drills, bulldozers, or pneumatic hammers to make the work easy, but they did have plenty of manpower. They had thousands of slaves to do the work, but even so, it took twenty years to complete the beautiful structure.

When finished, Sostratus' white marble masterpiece with its gleaming white columns soared four hundred feet from the middle of a huge courtyard whose many galleries, arcades, and gardens were lined with notable works of art. The three-story tower had a large square base about one hundred feet wide, an eight-sided second story, and a tall, round, third story. Above it all, in a large brazier, a fire was kept burning all the time. By day it poured out a huge column of smoke. By night, its flaming fire could be seen, it was said, for thirty miles.

A statue of the God of the Sea, Poseidon, stood on the top above the brazier, with his trident or three-pointed spear in one hand. Legend has it that he held a large mirror in the other hand, a mirror so clear that enemy vessels would be sighted in it while they were still over a hundred leagues away. Since a league is about three miles, this tale is a little hard to swallow. We do know, however, that the overall effect was one of grandeur, for Caesar, who visited Cleopatra in Alexandria in 48 B.C., spoke of the tower's great height and remarkable construction — and the Roman Caesars were not easily impressed.

The twenty years taken to build the lighthouse were well invested, for it lasted 1600 years. In A.D. 1349 it was found in ruins and no one knows to this day whether the conquering Turks destroyed it, an earthquake leveled it, or some mysterious power caused its collapse.

The architect Sostratus wanted credit for his work but evidently thought the king might not like sharing the honor. So he cut his name in the marble, then covered it with a softer material which would eventually wear off to reveal an inscription for all to read after both king and architect were dead and buried: SOSTRATUS OF CNIDUS son of DIXPHAUS to the Gods protecting those upon the sea.

The Arabs later made a half-hearted attempt to rebuild the great lighthouse but nothing came of it. Today, all that is left of the world's first authentic lighthouse is the word "pharos." In France the word for lighthouse is *phare;* in Spain and Italy, *faro;* and even in England for some time a lighthouse was known as a pharos.

Colossus of Rhodes

Picture, if you can, a giant bronze figure of a man, as tall as a ten-story building, standing in the middle of the city — legs apart, feet planted firmly on opposite sides of the street, holding an uplifted torch — while all the traffic of a busy thoroughfare flows between his outstretched legs.

Not long after the Egyptians built the Pharos, the Greeks, who lived a little to the west on the opposite shore of the Mediterranean, erected just such a figure. But instead of being on land, it stood in the harbor of Rhodes straddling the channel, so that all ships entering or leaving the port had to sail between its legs.

What we know about the Colossus of Rhodes is mostly legend, for no writer of the period left a detailed description of it, and nothing remains of this great work. It was not exactly a light*house,* even though it did hold a light, but it was without a doubt the most unusual seamark ever erected. We can only guess what it was like inside, and wonder how the fuel for its fire was brought all the way up to the torch. There was probably some sort of stairway or system of ladders inside.

In any case, it must have been a glorious sight: a giant bronze statue of the Sun God, Helios, towering over all the ships in the harbor, the light from its blazing torch shining, unobstructed, far out to sea. For eighty years it stood there guarding the harbor, and then suddenly it was gone, shattered into a thousand pieces, it is said, by an earthquake. Perhaps so, but the final blow might have been struck by one of the many legendary Greek gods, Zeus, father of them all, with his thunderbolts, or Vulcan, the blacksmith with his hammer, angered by some mortal slight. Two thousand years later, another colossal figure holding a torch was erected; this time it was the figure of a woman and it stands on Liberty Island, formerly Bedloe's Island, in the harbor of New York. It is called the Statue of Liberty.

Caligula's Light

The Egyptians and the Greeks had both built memorable light-houses and now it was the Romans' turn, for to them belongs history's next great lighthouse, la Tour d'Orde or Caligula's Light. The Emperor Caligula built it in A.D. 40, high on a cliff above Boulogne on the coast of France, to mark the site of a Roman en-campment. The emperor's real name was Caius Caesar Germani-cus, but when he was a little child his parents dressed him in military boots and he soon acquired the nickname "Caligula," which means "Little Boots." This man with the childish nickname was one of the world's cruelest tyrants. He delighted in torture and execution, and some said he was insane. He once remarked that he wished all the people in the world had but one neck so that he could cut off all their heads at one blow. But instead, to almost everyone's delight, he himself was assassinated by a man named Chaerea.

The lighthouse Caligula built was originally a large, 8-sided tower, 192 feet high, having 12 stories, each one a foot and a half

less in height than the one below it. But when Henry VIII of England captured Boulogne in 1544, he converted it into a fort by building 4 bastions and a wall around it. As a fort it received some rough treatment, and although it was still there in 1664, it had been so badly damaged that, despite the fact that it was partially restored by the Emperor Charlemagne in 811, it was never used as a lighthouse again.

Tour de Cordouan

The Romans, who had marched triumphantly across Asia, Africa, and Europe and had invaded and conquered Britain, were not only great soldiers but also superb engineers and builders of roads, aqueducts, temples, and bridges. They built lighthouses wherever they went, including a number on the southern coast of England.

When the Roman Empire finally collapsed and the Romans pulled up stakes and went home, their whole system of warning lights fell apart. A few fires were kept burning in church towers and monastery windows but their feeble glow gave almost no protection. The English coasts grew darker and more dangerous and, for several centuries, the wreckers who preyed on vessels in distress had things all their own way.

Meanwhile, across the channel, the French had succeeded in

doing what no one else had been able to do. They had built a lighthouse on a wave-swept site off shore. The Islet of Cordouan, one thousand yards long and half as wide, is a great reef in the Bay of Biscay near the city of Bordeaux; at high tide it is under water. Over two thousand lives have been lost in the vicinity of this "graveyard of ships." As early as the ninth century there was some sort of seamark here; and later the English, in control of the city, built a lighthouse with a platform forty-eight feet high on which a wood fire was kept burning. The citizens of Bordeaux, beginning the custom of "lighthouse dues" followed to this day, collected a small fee from each passing vessel.

The keeper of the light, a religious hermit, didn't mind being alone in this rickety lighthouse but when he died no one could be found to take the job. A new lighthouse was needed and one was started in 1584. And what a light! It took 26 years to build and no wonder, for it was most elaborate: part palace, part fort, part cathedral, and the rest lighthouse. Above a solid base, 135 feet around, were 4 circular stories. The first story contained a vast entrance hall and apartments for four keepers. The second was given over to the king's apartment, 2 luxurious chambers and a number of closets. The third story contained a magnificent chapel with a domed ceiling beautifully decorated in mosaic. It had not one, but two, lantern rooms, one above the other.

Keepers to live in this amazing tower were no trouble to find and, although the king never did come to call, and the chapel was unused except by the four keepers, the tower did its main job, saving lives, very well indeed.

The Tower of Hercules

The last of the truly ancient lights, the Tower of Hercules located at La Corunna, Spain, was built by the Phoenicians about A.D. 100. They built well, for the square 150-foot tower with its unusual outside staircase has been shining its beam there for more than 18 centuries. It was there when the Romans were occupying England and France; it was there when the Spanish Armada of 130 vessels and 30,000 men set forth from La Corunna in a disastrous attempt to invade England in 1588; and it was there on June 6, 1944, when the combined armed forces of the Allies sailed from England to land their liberating armies on the Normandy coast. It is the only one of the early lighthouses still in use.

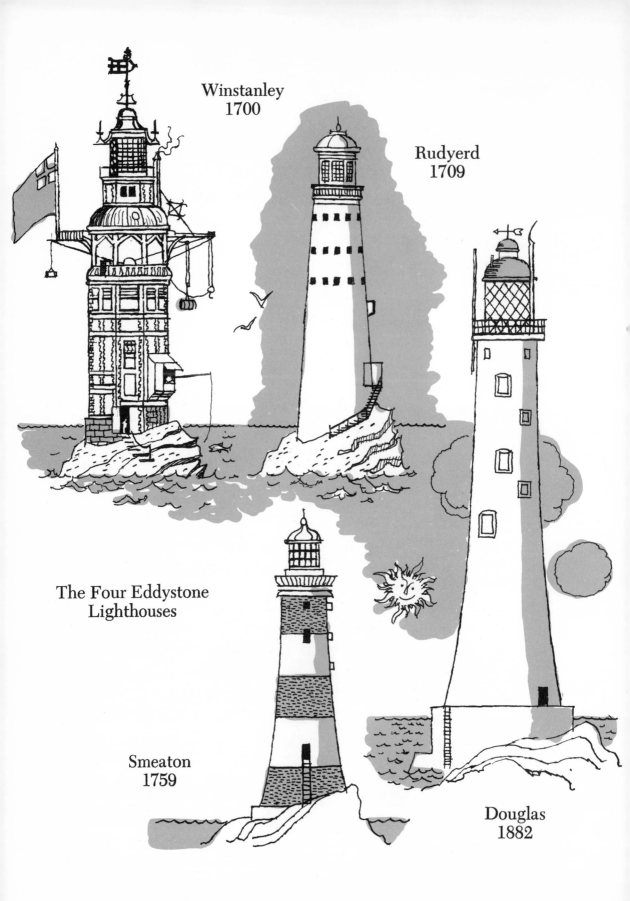

Winstanley
1700

Rudyerd
1709

Douglas
1882

The Four Eddystone
Lighthouses

Smeaton
1759

THE MOST FAMOUS LIGHTHOUSE IN THE WORLD

The Eddystone Light stands about fourteen miles southwest of
Plymouth on a small low-lying granite rock, whose highest point
is barely visible above the choppy waters of the English Channel.
Any vessel going into or out of Plymouth Harbor, to or from the
open ocean, has to pass this dangerous reef, and for centuries
English seafaring men have feared it and have been careful to
give it a wide berth. Captain Christopher Jones of the good ship
Mayflower, who sailed from Plymouth in 1620 with a shipload of
settlers for the New World, later wrote that he had "managed to
avoid" a "wicked reef of rust red rocks" which lay outside the
harbor. Others were not always so lucky, and in the years to
follow so many vessels were wrecked on the rocks that finally, in
1694, the government decided to build a lighthouse there.

Mr. Winstanley's Wonderful Tower

The job was given to Henry Winstanley, a very clever fellow: a
painter, an inventor, a businessman, a ship owner, and most of
all a showman. But he didn't know much about building light-

houses. He had a house in the country, a strange place, a crazy museum full of weird inventions, ghostly figures, trick furniture, and practical jokes of all kinds. He called it "Winstanley's Wonders" and he charged a shilling to go through it. He had another show in London, "Winstanley's Waterworkes," a series of spectacular arrangements of fire and water, of fountains, pools, and colored lights. So it is not surprising that the lighthouse he built turned out to be a little unusual too — just another of Winstanley's wonders. It was an amazing construction, a six-sided tower of stone and wood about one hundred feet high, heavily draped in iron hoisting gear, and plastered with balconies, balustrades, cornices, flagpoles, gold paint, and ornamental gadgets of every description.

Mr. Winstanley, pleased with his work, proudly predicted that it would last forever, but the local fishermen just shook their heads doubtfully and kept their fingers crossed. During the winter storms it swayed alarmingly and much of the ornamental work blew away, but the tower was still standing in the spring. For three more years its light shone brightly and, best of all, no ships were lost on the dreaded rocks. Then in November, 1703, the worst storm England had ever known hit the coast. The wind blew at a gale force for two weeks without a sign of stopping, causing tremendous damage everywhere. When a lull finally came, Mr. Winstanley rushed out to check his tower. He arrived there all right, but before he could start back the storm struck again. The wind blew harder than ever, tossing the ships in the harbor into a tangled mass of crushed hulls and splintered spars. One hundred and fifty ships were sunk and eight thousand sailors lost their lives. Rivers everywhere overran their banks, flooding the countryside and drowning thousands of sheep, goats, and other livestock. The furious wind bowled over church steeples, mowed down giant oaks, and lifted the roofs off cottage and castle alike, filling the air with flying tiles and chimney pots. Everyone ran for cover, hiding in closets, and crawling under beds. Even the queen and the ladies of the Court were forced to seek safety in the palace cellar.

The storm struck on Friday, the twentieth of November, and lasted throughout the night. Saturday morning the wind died down, the sun shone again, and the waters were calm. But Henry Winstanley, his companions, and his wonderful lighthouse were gone forever.

The Second Tower

Mr. Winstanley had shown not only that a lighthouse could be built on a wave-covered rock, he had shown how not to build one; and when John Rudyerd designed the second tower, he was careful to avoid making the same mistakes. In order to offer less resistance to the elements, Rudyerd built a round tower with a smooth, unbroken surface from top to bottom. To make sure that it would be strong enough, he used interlocking blocks of granite and timber, anchored it firmly to the reef with thirty-six iron rods driven deep in the rock, and for extra reinforcement added a mast running up the middle like a backbone. So far, so good, and for forty-six years it stood guard on the Eddystone rocks, unharmed by wind or wave. But an enemy lurked inside the walls, and on the night of December 1, 1755, the enemy struck — *fire!*

On that night, when Henry Hall, ninety-four years of age and the oldest of the three keepers, opened the lantern room door on his regular inspection tour, he was met by a burst of smoke and flame. He grabbed a bucket, filled it with water from the tank outside on the balcony, and emptied it onto the fire, all the while shouting for help. Back and forth he went in a desperate effort to put out the blaze. By the time the others arrived the water was about gone, and the three men were forced to back down under a shower of flaming bits of timber and white-hot metal. Suddenly

Henry, choking and gasping for air, collapsed in a heap on the floor, moaning that he had swallowed a piece of molten metal. It was hard to believe that the old man had swallowed such a thing, but in any case there was nothing the others could do except carry him out onto the rocks to a spot as far away as possible from the blazing tower. Here all three clung, wet, scorched, and exhausted, until rescuers arrived the next morning.

Twelve days later when old Mr. Hall died, it seemed as if he had been telling the truth. Dr. Henry Spry who examined him found a seven-ounce piece of lead, shaped as though poured into a mould, resting in the pit of his stomach. All that was left of the tower were some twisted iron rods and a few blocks of granite. Once again, the reef was free to claim its victims.

The Third Tower

But not for long. Just one year later, the job of building another lighthouse was given to John Smeaton. It was a wise choice, for Smeaton was an engineer and knew what he was doing. This time there were no mistakes. His tower, like Rudyerd's, was round and smooth, but taller and with sides gently curving inward from bottom to top. He built it entirely of dovetailed granite blocks, fastened together with marble plugs and oaken nails, so that, to all intents and purposes, the tower was one piece of granite, fireproof and more solid than even the rock supporting it. It stood there guarding the approach to Plymouth for almost one hundred and twenty years until, in 1878, the ledge beneath it was found to be crumbling away and it was decided to erect a new and taller light on a more solid section of rock.

The citizens of Plymouth did not want to part with their faithful old watchdog and they paid to have it dismantled and reassembled in the town where every one could see it. It's big eye is blinded now, but the gaily painted structure is the center of attraction, a favorite meeting place of young and old alike, and a lasting tribute to the genius of the first lighthouse engineer, Thomas Smeaton.

The Fourth Tower

Each new lighthouse had been an improvement over the one before it and Sir James Douglas's tower was no exception, especially since he had much more modern equipment than any of the earlier builders: pneumatic rock drills, powerful cranes and pumps, and a greatly improved quick-drying cement. He also had a twin screw steamer, *Hercules*, which anchored nearby and served as a floating hotel and workshop. Even with all these advantages, it took four years to build his lighthouse, for this was by far the largest of the Eddystone lights. The site he chose was under water all the time and, in order to build the base, his men had to work in a cofferdam, a circular shield resembling a can with open ends. One end rests on the sea bottom while the other end rises well above

the waterline. Once it is in place and the water is pumped out, the men inside it can keep dry while working below the surface.

Sir James followed Smeaton's design very closely, the only difference being that he made his tower taller and placed it in the middle of a solid, round platform with vertical sides that reached almost three feet above the waterline. This platform made a four-foot landing area around the tower and also served to break up waves before they could run up the tower and damage the light.

The 9-story, 140-foot stone tower, with a huge 7-ton oil-burning lantern on top, was finished in 1882; and, except for changing from oil to electricity, it remains untouched to this day, visible proof that, after 200 years and 4 attempts, the red rocks of Eddystone have finally been conquered.

LIGHTHOUSES AND HOW THEY WORK

THE STORY OF the lighthouse in this country begins with the building of Boston Light by the Massachusetts Bay colonists back in 1716. It was not only America's first lighthouse, it was also typical of those which were to follow for the next hundred years or so. How it came to be built and what happened to it makes fascinating reading but, before we talk about that and a number of other thrilling tales of famous lighthouses and their keepers, let's take a look at the lighthouse of today to find out what makes it work.

The Different Kinds

The lighthouse builders of those early Colonial days always put their beacons on land, atop a cliff or a hill overlooking the sea, where materials were close at hand and the actual building presented no problem. They were usually made of rubble stone masonry or brick, although occasionally a wooden tower would be added to a keeper's cottage. This last method was the simplest of all but risky, for wood catches fire easily, and there was always the danger, too, that a really strong wind would rip off the tower and blow out the light. On at least one occasion that's exactly what did happen.

Since iron lasts longer than wood and is only a little more costly than brick, that metal was often used in building early lighthouses. The ones at Cape Henry and at Parris Island, South Carolina, were both iron towers.

In the early 1900's, a big change in the method of constructing lighthouses occurred when the San Francisco earthquake of 1906 destroyed the Point Arena Light. It was rebuilt using reinforced concrete for the first time in a lighthouse. It proved to be such a great success that this building material is today by far the most popular for lighthouse construction.

Land-based lighthouses which mark the approaches to harbors and enable a navigator to figure out where he is at all times are certainly a great help, but they cannot provide safety from the greatest danger to shipping: the submerged rocks and shoals out in the open sea a long way from land. Building bases solid enough to support heavy towers on these wind and wave-swept sites is a much more difficult and dangerous task than building on land, and the Americans were too busy establishing themselves and gaining independence to do much about this problem until about 1850.

When they did get around to it, they found that one of three methods would almost always work. Where the bare rock was exposed they could cut, fit, and cement the massive stone blocks of the foundation to steps cut in the rock, as was done at the famous Eddystone Light. Where the rock was not far below a layer of mud or sand, either a coffer dam could be built on the site which could then be filled with rock or concrete, or a steel cylinder called a caisson could be floated to the spot, sunk, the sand and mud inside around the bottom blown out with powerful jets of water, and the steel shell filled with masonry to make one solid hunk of stone resting on bedrock. This is the way the lighthouse was built at Fourteen Foot Bank in Delaware Bay.

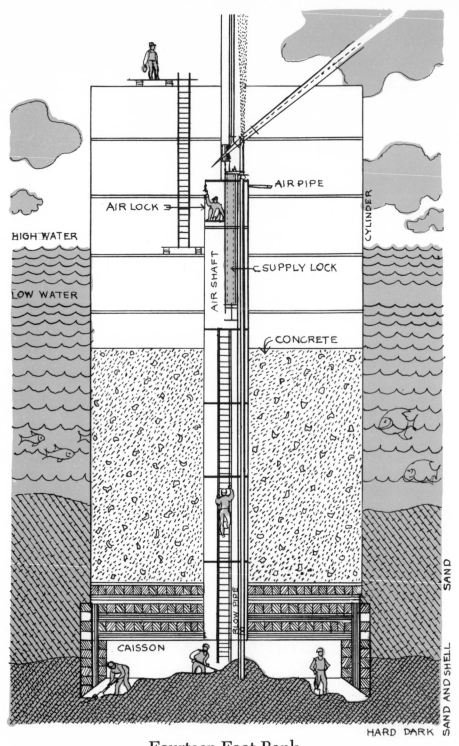

HIGH WATER

LOW WATER

AIR LOCK

AIR PIPE

CYLINDER

AIR SHAFT

SUPPLY LOCK

CONCRETE

BLOW PIPE

SAND

CAISSON

SAND AND SHELL

HARD DARK

Fourteen Foot Bank

Where the bottom consisted of sand, gravel, or coral with no rock beneath, iron piles could be driven into the softer soil, sometimes as much as one hundred feet, as a foundation for an openwork iron tower. These skeleton towers were cheaper to build than the solid ones and had the added advantage of offering less resistance to the tremendous force of the waves and the battering of drifting ice. One of these, Cape Charles Light, is at the entrance to Chesapeake Bay, placed there in 1895. On land, too, where the sod is too damp or too loose and shifting to support a stone lighthouse, these skeleton towers are the answer to the problem.

Identifying a Lighthouse

A lighthouse has two jobs to do regardless of whether it is made of brick, stone, or iron, is perched on a headland, or has its base deep beneath the waves. It must warn ships away from the immediate danger of rocks or shoals, and must tell the navigator where he is. And it must do this under any weather conditions and from as great a distance as possible. Obviously, the first thing to do to accomplish this is to put the lighthouse somewhere where it can be seen, and that is why so many early ones were placed on high bluffs or hills near the sea. But seeing a lighthouse from the deck of a ship is not enough, for if the navigator cannot tell which beacon he sees he cannot be sure where he is, and that can lead to trouble.

By day there are several ways to tell. If it is shore based, one may recognize a lighthouse by the character of the landscape

around it; and whether it is on land or at sea, there is the overall size and shape and other architectural details, such as the placing of windows, doors, and balconies, to help identify it. What catches the eye first, though, when one looks at a lighthouse is the pattern of bright colors and bold design that makes each different from all the others. Unfortunately, none of these things is any help at night when there is only the beam of the light itself to go by. Just as "all cats are grey at night," all lights are pretty much alike in the dark, and if there are several in the same area it is almost impossible to tell one from another. If every light were a different color, identification would be no problem. The trouble with color is that the loss of light through colored glass is enormous — as much as 70 percent through a red lens — and because of this weakness, colors have to be used sparingly, mostly in channels and harbors where the light does not have to carry very far.

The solution is to use a flashing beam and to give each light a different pattern of on and off periods, so that a navigator with a chart describing the flash sequence and a stop watch can check the light and dark periods and tell almost immediately which light is signaling. This system is called either *occulting* or *flashing:* occulting if the light periods are equal to or greater than the dark periods, flashing if the dark periods are greater. At first, this flashing effect was produced by placing a number of lamps at fixed intervals on a circular framework which was then revolved. The revolving machinery was controlled by a weight-operated clockwork mechanism. As the framework slowly revolved, the light would appear as a series of flashes which could be varied by placing the lamps at different intervals on the wheel. It worked, after a fashion, but it was awfully slow, and the intervals between flashes were too long. The process worked somewhat better when the light was made stationary and a lens with panels was revolved around it; it worked a great deal better when, in 1890, a way was found to float the heavy lens mounting, weighing about seven tons, on a circular trough of mercury. Mercury is so dense that it can easily support this great weight, and as it is almost friction-free, the touch of a finger is enough to start the whole ponderous contraption moving and revolving at a much faster rate, making possible a tremendous number of different flash patterns. Now it was possible for each lighthouse to have its own flash signal, made up of a series of light and dark dots and dashes, a sort of Morse code in light instead of sound.

Fuel for the Flame

Light control was certainly a great step forward, but while all these advances were being made, even greater things were happening to the design of the lamp. And every time the lamp was changed, the fuel had to be changed too.

The very first coastal beacons, the bonfires blazing on hilltops thousands of years ago, undoubtedly burned wood; and the ancient Egyptians used bitumen or pitch in their pots and braziers along the Nile. For a long time, a thousand years or so, these two fuels, pitch and wood, were generally used.

Then, around 1560, the Swedes started using coal. Coal burns very well but it gives off more heat than light and a lighthouse keeper, naturally enough, is interested only in getting the greatest amount of light possible. Candles, on the other hand, give relatively more light than heat, and as each candle produces the same amount of light as every other candle of the same size, it is a simple matter to make up a beam of the desired brightness. That is why candles soon became the favored fuel and that is why, even with today's unlimited electrical power on tap, the lights are graded according to their candle power.

Incidentally, the Scots were still burning coal in a Scottish lighthouse as late as 1816, long after everyone else had turned to other fuels. But the Scots probably had a large supply of coal on hand.

The first really important step forward in lamp design came in 1782 when a Swiss named Argand invented a lamp which made use of a circular wick with a current of air passing through its center. This lamp burned oil and gave a much brighter and steadier flame than anything used so far.

A great many different kinds of oil were burned — vegetable, animal and mineral, whale, fish, colza, lard — all had their turn as rising costs made one or the other too expensive. Although kerosene, distilled from coal, turned out to be a better fuel than any of the vegetable or animal oils, it was for a long time thought to be too dangerous to use, especially after one keeper on Lake Michigan who decided to try it blew up his lantern and almost killed himself doing it. It burned so much better than anything else, however, that a way was soon found to make it safe, and by 1855 everyone was using it.

The next great advance was a lamp in which the kerosene, under pressure, was heated until it became vapor, mixed with air, and burned under a mantle. The mantle, made of gauze and impregnated with metallic oxides, was invented by Carl von Welsbach, an Austrian chemist. His combination of lamp and mantle gave about eight times as much light as the wick lamp and used less oil. It was this method that was used to light peoples' houses prior to the invention of the electric light bulb. Coal oil gas, gas made from rosin, acetylene gas, and natural gas all worked well in the Welsbach burner. Meanwhile, experiments with electricity had been going on, and in 1886 an electric arc light was placed in the Statue of Liberty. Three years later, the Sandy Hook beacon at the entrance to New York Harbor was also electrified.

It remained for Thomas A. Edison, inventor of the phonograph,

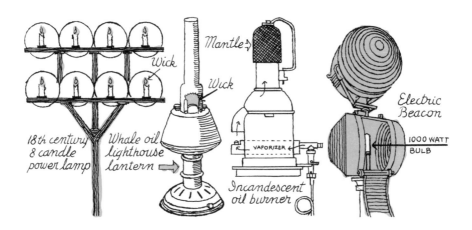

to revolutionize the world's lighting by perfecting the first practical electric incandescent bulb. This new form of light was in-
credibly bright, so bright it almost seemed as though the sun itself
had been harnessed and put to work in the lighthouse tower. All
this power wasn't really needed but it was comforting to know it
was there, and soon all the major shore-based lights were electrified. But not the ocean lights; the keepers dared not count on an
uninterrupted flow of current from distant power stations, particularly as the current had to travel long distances through underwater cables along the bottom of the sea. They had to wait until
the invention of the compact Diesel generator, which enabled
them to make their own electricity, before taking advantage of this
wonderful source of power. What will come next is anybody's
guess. It may well be an atom-powered, pocket-size generator,
although we may have to wait a few years for that.

The Lens and the Light

Light rays fan out in all directions from their source so that whatever light is not directed to the spot where it is needed, is wasted.
A bonfire on shore meant to guide ships into port sends almost
half its light behind it where it does no good at all. Down through
the centuries, engineers and lighting experts have been working
on ways to capture this elusive light and put it to work. The first
thing they did was to put the flame inside a lantern made of heavy
metal, with small glass panes to protect it from the wind and rain.
The lantern protected the flame all right but did not do anything
to increase the power of the light, so they placed a shiny reflector
behind it. This was the first attempt to corral some of the wasted
light and direct it to a given spot. Later reflectors were cone-
shaped or parabolic and not only reflected the rays but formed
them into single streams or beams of light. This method of re-
flection is known as the *catoptric* method.

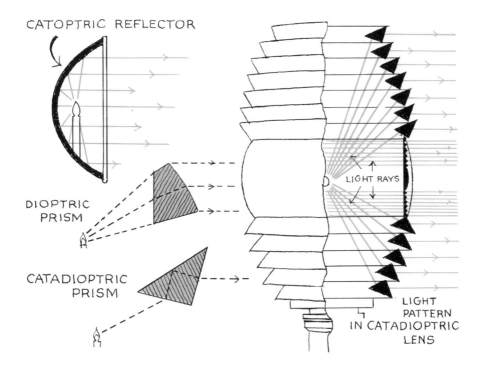

CATOPTRIC REFLECTOR

DIOPTRIC PRISM

CATADIOPTRIC PRISM

LIGHT RAYS

LIGHT PATTERN IN CATADIOPTRIC LENS

Too much of the light was still escaping at the top, bottom, and sides, however, and more of this was saved by placing prism-shaped lenses all around the light. These lenses bend the light rays passing through them and send them out in a different direction to join the others in making a beam. This method of bending or refracting light is called the *dioptric* method.

In 1822, Augustin Fresnel combined both methods in his Fresnel lens, an apparatus built of a central spherical lens surrounded by several rings of glass prisms so arranged that they both reflect and refract, gathering in most of the light rays and focusing them into one solid, greatly magnified column of blazing light. Naturally enough, this became known as the *catadioptric* method. Fresnel's huge apparatus, ten feet high and six feet wide, with its intricate arrangement of lenses and glass prisms surrounding the powerful light like a cage, is a beautiful thing to look at when the light is off. When it is on, no man dares look, any more than he could stare into the face of the sun.

There is still some loss of light at top and bottom and by absorption in the glass, but, thanks to Mr. Fresnel and Mr. Edison, the power of the lights has risen beyond belief. Where it was once measured in terms of a dozen or so candle flames, today's beam is equal to the combined brightness of millions, with almost no limit to the possible candle power. Before this great jump in power, lighthouses were classified as first-, second-, or third-order lights, according to the focal length of the lens, the focal length being the distance from the center of the light to the lens's inner surface. The first order had a focal length of thirty-six inches, the second twenty-seven inches, and the third twenty inches. Now they are all rated by their candle power, which gives a much better idea of the intensity of the light.

The Voice of the Lighthouse

No matter how powerful the light, there have always been times when a vessel has had to rely on hearing to get warning of danger. Wrapped in a blanket of fog, a ship is blind, and until fairly recently, the only warning a helmsman would sometimes receive would be the terrifying sound — often too late to save his vessel — of the waves breaking on rocks. As a result, many types of fog signals were tried out. At Boston Light in 1719, a cannon was fired during a heavy fog, but only in answer to a similar signal from a vessel seeking help. The cannon idea did not work very well and Boston soon gave it up. San Francisco tried it later but abandoned the cannon, too, in 1855. For a time it seemed that a bell would be the answer and West Quoddy Light in Maine, where the fog is about as bad as anywhere, was the first to have one.

But problems arose here too. For one thing, a bell has to be rung by hand, for although some big ones weighing as much as two tons and run by clockwork were tried out, they were too unreliable. It was hand ringing or nothing. Even with extra pay, the light-

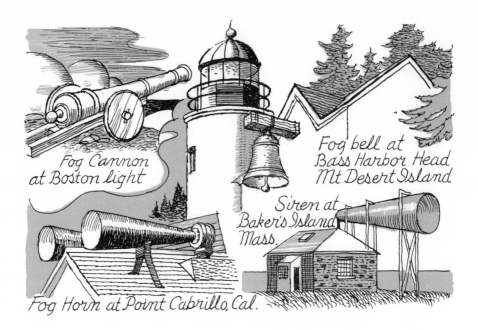

Fog Cannon at Boston light

Fog bell at Bass Harbor Head Mt. Desert Island

Siren at Baker's Island Mass.

Fog Horn at Point Cabrillo, Cal.

house keepers, to a man, took a dim view of this chore. The bell warning that worked best consisted of a small boat, completely decked over to make it watertight, with a bell hung loosely inside so that the motion of the waves kept it rocking and ringing. A number of these bell ships were moored at various danger points all along the coast where they gave the general impression of a tethered whale which had swallowed a gong. Unfortunately, when not breaking their mooring chains, too often they were being sunk by vessels unable to tell from their sound how far away they were. Nonetheless, the idea was generally considered a good one as you can see by the great numbers of bell buoys that dot our harbors and coastal waters.

With each massive source of sound — cannon, bell, horn, and steam whistle — the noise grew louder and clearer. Still the search for a more penetrating sound continued until someone discovered a new type of noise machine, the siren. The siren's piercing wail is caused by jets of compressed air, forced into a round metal plate revolving around another plate similarly slotted. This causes it to howl like a banshee or, banshees being rare, like a fire engine or a police car.

The diaphone, a variation of the siren, has the same two cylinders which instead of being spun, are moved rapidly forward and backward, in a reciprocating instead of rotary motion. The blasts of sound the diaphone produces are literally earth-shaking. Their vibrations not only shake buildings but actually set off landslides.

Another type of horn, the diaphragm horn, has a disk in its throat which, when vibrated by jets of compressed air or electronic impulses directed at its center, adds yet another ear-splitting note to the collection of clangs, howls, shrieks, whistles, and roars that blast out their warnings whenever the fog rolls in.

Electronic Signals

Mother Nature is a mischievous old dame who likes to play tricks with sound waves, using heat, snow, rain, and other atmospheric conditions to distort and silence them. For instance, a good strong wind can bounce sound waves up and push them down, sometimes producing great gaps in the path of the signal so that it can't be heard at all. Any vessel relying on it is apt to get into trouble or at least be temporarily lost. As long as vessels had to rely on the sound of bell or horn to tell them where they were, they never could be absolutely sure of their positions. The radio wave which came along in the early 1900's was much more reliable, although it too was subject to some distortion. The early shipboard wireless, which enabled men on distant ships to talk to each other and to

shore stations, was a great comfort, especially in case of emergencies. It didn't help much, though, in getting a fix on a ship's position. The radio compass and direction finder, developed in the First World War, was a step in the right direction, for a radio beam is like an invisible railroad track stretching ahead of a ship into the distance. If you follow it, you will arrive safely at its end. The radio direction finder made it a simple matter to stay on the track. It works like this: A loop antenna, mounted above the pilot house, picks up the signal from a lighthouse or lightship and magnifies it. The loop keeps turning around, and as the sound is loudest when the plane of the loop is facing the sender and keeps getting weaker as it turns away, the direction of the sender is clearly indicated by the volume of the sound.

This radio compass could be counted on to point the way to the lighthouse, but it couldn't say how far away it was, and that was terribly important. It wasn't too difficult though, to work that out, Since radio waves travel much faster than sound waves, a radio signal and a diaphone sound signal sent from a lighthouse at the same instant will arrive at any given point at different times. If the two signals are sent out at regular, specified intervals so that the starting time is known, the navigator on the bridge with a stop watch can measure the difference in travel time. The radio signal travels at 186,000 miles a second and is almost instantaneous, but the sound wave travels only a mile in five seconds. All the navigator has to do to tell how far he is from the sender is divide the time difference between the two signals (in seconds) by five. For instance, if the time difference is thirty seconds, dividing it by five would give six as the answer — the difference in miles from the sender. Cross bearings on two or more stations within a two hundred mile radius will give a vessel's position, for once you know how far you are from two or more fixed points, your own is established. Knowing its position at all times spells safety for a ship at sea, and the radio wave has at last made that possible.

Airports depend on radar to keep track of air traffic. Straight lines show routes, Xs are check points, and circles indicate range in miles. Planes appear as irregular "blips"

Radar, which first played an important part in the Battle of Britain in World War II by giving warning of the presence of enemy ships and planes, is useful in times of peace, too. Like a rubber ball bouncing back from a brick wall, or an echo resounding from a mountain side, a radio signal sent from a ship, plane, or other station, will, if it bumps into any solid object, bounce back and register a blip on a screen. Since the direction of the radio signal is known, the sender is warned of the presence of an object in his path and can take appropriate action.

Sonar is the underwater version of radar, used often by submarines during the war to ferret out their enemy counterparts. Instead of seeing a blip on a screen, the operator, wearing headphones, listens for a ping which means, "look out, enemy sub ahead." It wasn't always a submarine that caused the sonar ping. Sometimes the enemy turned out to be nothing more dangerous

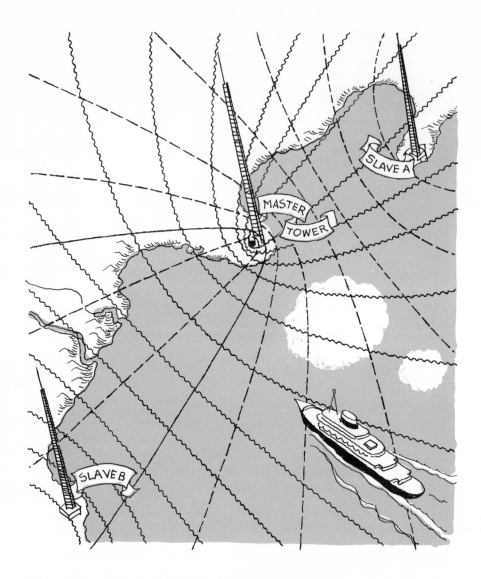

than a lone whale peacefully cruising along with no other thought in mind than where his next meal was coming from.

The wireless, the radio beam and compass, radar, and sonar have all played their part in making navigation safe. Now loran, the long range navigation system developed in the Second World War, has made navigation even safer and easier. Unlike radar, the loran system does not involve transmission from the ship; and the signal, instead of being continuous, is made up of a series of short bursts of energy, giving it a pulsing, throbbing beat. And unlike ordinary radio waves which are subject to some distortion as they cross land areas from the sea, the loran signal is constant and indestructible. The long range navigation system relies on the measurement of the difference in distance of a vessel to two points whose positions are known to the navigator. The heart of the system is a series of tall steel skeleton towers which operate in "threes", a master tower controlling two "slaves" which broadcast signals from positions anywhere from two hundred miles to six hundred miles apart. These signals can be identified by their distinctive pulse beats, and since the navigator knows the positions of the sending stations, the rate of travel of the signals, and the difference in arrival times, he can determine his ship's position in relation to the two stations. A machine looking much like a small television receiver does most of the work. It receives the signals, records the times of arrival, figures out the difference between them, and shows the result on a direct-reading indicator. With this information, the navigator refers to his chart, finds the appropriate spot marked on it, and, since the chart also gives latitude and longitude, his exact position is clearly indicated. The most wonderful thing about loran is that nothing can affect its accuracy. And its great range, up to two thousand miles, means that a few loran stations can do the work of a great many lighthouses.

The Anatomy of the Lighthouse

No doubt about it, loran really does the job, and as more and more of the steel skeleton towers appear along our shores charting the atmosphere with their invisible highways, it becomes increasingly clear that, after several thousand years of loyal service, the lighthouse as we know it will go the way of the pony express, the clipper ship, and the iron horse. Before they disappear entirely, let's look at a cross section of one of these wonderful towers to see what goes on inside.

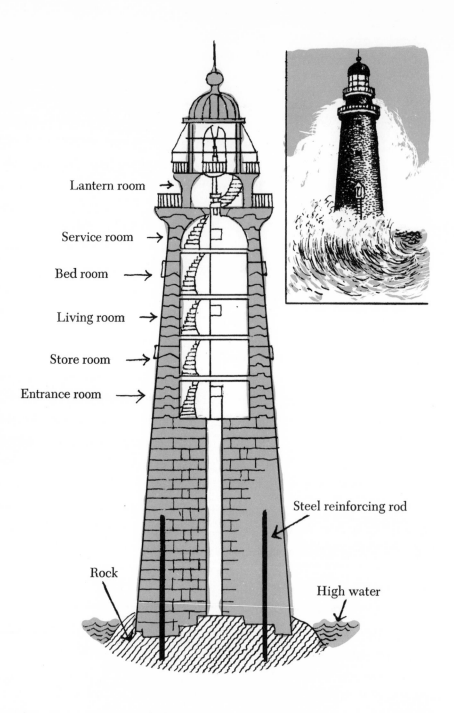

Lantern room →

Service room →

Bed room →

Living room →

Store room →

Entrance room →

Steel reinforcing rod

Rock

High water

This one is typical of the offshore beacons such as Eddystone or Minot's. Above its rocky, wave-swept foundation is a central well. Then come six rooms, one above the other. These are storage rooms, living quarters, service rooms, and, above all, a lantern room. The great flashing light with its central lens surrounded by thousands of glass prisms looking like petals on a crystal flower, is the most intricate and vital part of the whole structure. This huge assembly, fifteen feet tall and weighing seven or eight tons, floats on a bed of mercury, a complicated set-up that has been tended and watched over by generations of dedicated men and women who often spent their whole lives in its service.

Now that the electronic age has changed all this, and the really modern lighthouse is practically self-reliant, depending less and less on light and sound and more and more on electronic signals, it has no need for a keeper in constant attendance; instead it seems to have become almost human itself.

It has a skeleton of steel covered by a skin of granite. Deep inside, a compact power generator feeds on a diet of Diesel oil and, like a steadily beating heart, pumps its electrical life blood along the arteries of wire and cable running from head to toe throughout the body. Like man, its head is held high. Inside it are the eye, vocal cords, and the electronic brain, controlling the whole complicated system of light and sound, a brain which can even make corrections if anything should go wrong. Add a nervous system made up of an intricate network of fine insulated wires to carry the messages from the computer brain to the organ of sight and sound, and you can readily see that lighthouses and men do have much in common — including the fact that they are both mortal and doomed to die.

It seems too bad to see the old lighthouses go, even though loran does a better job of protecting shipping, for it is hard to work up much feeling for a few skeleton towers several hundred miles apart, that appear to stand there making no sound and showing no light. Perhaps some day a collection of romantic tales will develop around the loran service. Meanwhile, we can be sure that the stories and legends of the lighthouses and the brave band of "Wickies" who served them so faithfully will live forever.

THE ROCK BOUND COAST

WE WILL BEGIN with Maine since it is the most easterly of these United States, and work westward to the shores of the Pacific. Much of Maine is, so far, unspoiled by the hand of man. It is a land of mountain, river, lake, and forest. In a coloring book you would color it green and blue — green because three-quarters of its land is covered by a carpet of pine, spruce, and hemlock, and blue because of the more than two thousand lakes that are scattered throughout its 33,215 square miles. It is a land of clear blue days and crisp cool nights, of strong fresh winds, and white clouds across a summer sky, a land where the mountains meet the sea and the great dark forest carpeting the land seems to be marching down to the water's edge in an effort to push back the incoming tides that ceaselessly beat against the rocky shores.

Maine is beautiful, a fisherman's delight, and for the sailing enthusiast it is Heaven itself. Its long irregular coastline indented with bays, river mouths, and coves, together with the hundreds of islands sprinkled like jewels all along its length, combine to make it the country's favorite cruising ground. The only real drawback is the fog that frequently settles down over land and sea like a wet blanket, hiding all the familiar landmarks from sight so that the whole world seems to have melted away.

But most of all, when we think of Maine, we think of the sea itself, the deep, cold, clear waters of the North Atlantic, the surging tides that rise and fall as much as twenty feet, and the pounding waves throwing up their white plumes against the age-old rocks lining the shore. And we think, too, of the hardy and resourceful men and women who settled here in the first place, hoping to make their living tilling the soil as they had always done. They soon found that the soil was poor, the growing season short, and farming wasn't practical. So they turned their attention to the ocean, which was right at their doorstep, full of enough food to feed a thousand times their number. The herring, mackerel, scallops, cod, and lobsters were there for the taking and Maine's residents soon became expert fishermen, shipbuilders, and sailors.

Since so much of their life was spent on the sea and their whole livelihood depended on it, the people of Maine could have been expected to lead the way in lighthouse building. However, they must have been such good navigators that they did not need anything to guide them, for Boston had a lighthouse at the entrance to its harbor in 1716, almost three quarters of a century before Maine built her first one at Portland Head in 1787. A great many more have been built since then and today twenty-nine major beacons and one lightship are strung out along the coast beginning at the most easterly point, West Quoddy Head, up near Canada's Campobello Island where President Franklin D. Roosevelt spent his vacations.

West Quoddy Head

It's rugged country up around Quoddy: mostly forest, rocks, and water, with jagged headlands reaching far out into the ocean, a place of strong winds and tremendous tides, of battering surf, and of fog that sometimes lasts for days. It is just the place for a lighthouse, and in 1808, during President Thomas Jefferson's administration, one was built at the tip of West Quoddy Head. It seems odd that at first the lighthouse had no fog warning and did not get one until twelve years later when a bell was installed. The keeper had to ring this bell by hand and, as in this very foggy land it meant a lot of extra work, he asked for more money. He got it, but only after seven years of correspondence with Washington; and when it did come the raise was only sixty dollars a year.

From time to time the bell was changed. There were five in all, each one larger than the previous one, the last weighing over a thousand pounds. Nowadays, of course, instead of a bell, West Quoddy has a diaphone horn and a radio beacon in addition to its flashing white light, to warn the fogbound mariner. It is a colorful lighthouse. It isn't always foggy here, and when the sun shines on the tower it looks, with its gay red and white horizontal stripes, for all the world like a great candy cane.

Mount Desert

It is only three hundred miles from Eastport at one end of the Maine coast to Kittery at the other; that is, if you don't count all the ins and outs of the many river outlets and bays. If you do, the coast is closer to 2500 miles and most of it is hard, unyielding granite that can crush like an eggshell the hull of the stoutest vessel. To add to the danger, the waters are full of rocks and shoals. And always lurking in the background is the menace of fog which comes stealing in without warning to blot out all signs.

Mount Desert Light (pronounced *dessert*, like the sweet at the end of a meal), first in the Coast Guard's list of lights, is located on a half acre of barren rock out in the open sea about seventy miles southwest of West Quoddy and twenty miles directly south of Mt. Desert Island, in one of the most dangerous spots along the coast. This rock rises a bare seventeen feet above the surface of the ocean so that even on a clear day it might not be seen in time, especially if the water were at all rough. In foggy weather there is no chance of seeing the rock at all. Fog is certainly bad enough, but the winter storms are worse, and this storm-battered rock is no stranger to disaster.

There was the night the seagoing tug *Astral*, with a barge in tow, went aground on one of the ledges. Despite the raging seas and icy December blasts, the two keepers managed to heave a line to the stricken vessel and haul eighteen half-frozen men to safety through the breakers. They actually rescued only seventeen men because the eighteenth was dead when they pulled him in.

And there were many other nights, and days too, when gale-driven vessels were hurled upon the rocks and lives hung in the balance.

But Mount Desert wasn't always dark and forbidding. In the days when the keeper and his family lived on the rock, it was the custom each spring for the people on the mainland to carry bags of soil out to the lighthouse. They stuffed this soil into all the nooks and crannies of the rocks and then planted flower seeds so that, for a short time in summer, the bleak rocky landscape would blossom out in patches of brilliant color. Every winter the wind would blow away all the sod, leaving nothing but the bare rock again. Nowadays Mt. Desert, like so many of the outer beacons, is automatic and no one bothers to plant flowers there anymore.

Great Duck Island

Directly to the north of Mt. Desert Light, between it and the island of Mt. Desert, lies another of Maine's major beacons, Great Duck Island Light. Unlike its neighbor to the south, Great Duck Island does have some growing things on it, enough to have kept one man alive for several years. In the days before there was a light on the island, a ship was wrecked off nearby Little Duck Island. Most of the crew were drowned, but one fellow was a strong swimmer and he made it to Great Duck where, like Robinson Crusoe, he built himself a hut and, by eating roots and berries and whatever sea creatures he could catch, managed to keep himself from starving. When he was finally rescued, he had to be captured like a wild animal, for he was as frightened of his rescuers as a fawn. He had been alone so long that he had even forgotten how to speak. The story ends happily, though, for eventually the poor man did recover and go back to his overjoyed family.

In the days of the shipwrecked sailor, the island had a population of one, and it didn't grow very fast even after a lighthouse was built. At one point, however, Great Duck's population reached a total of eighteen. This wasn't a great number but, considering the fact that they were all members of the same family, it wasn't bad. There was the keeper, Nathan Reed, his wife, Emma, and sixteen little Reeds. This was probably a world's record for the number of children of one family living in one lighthouse. A schoolhouse had to be built on the island to take care of the Reed children. The teacher was the oldest girl, Rena, who had graduated from a school on the mainland and gone back to the island to be with her sisters and brothers. Mr. Reed was transferred to another post in 1912 and the school was discontinued for lack of pupils. The light, though, is still there, its 30,000 candle power red beam flashing out every ten seconds over the cold Atlantic waters.

Matinicus

Some forty miles farther west we come to Matinicus Island. Directly south of it and five miles away lies a rock. It is a big rock, thirty acres of solid granite — a lifeless place where nothing grows: no trees, no bushes, no flowers, no grass, nothing — plunked down in the open sea twenty-two miles off Penobscot Bay. The coast of Maine is not called rock bound without good reason and skippers and navigators sailing in those waters can thank the U.S. Coast Guard for the many guiding beacons like the one on Matinicus Rock which are scattered all along its rugged shores. It is a lonely spot. Until a light was placed there in 1827, gulls, terns, seals, and that rare bird the puffin were its only visitors.

At first the lighthouse had twin towers of wood and wooden dwellings. These suffered so much damage from winter storms that they were eventually replaced by stone towers and houses. The light is automatic now and no women live there, but back

in 1856 when Sam Burgess was the keeper, there were five; for Sam had a wife, who was rather sickly, and four daughters. He also had a grown son who spent little time at the light.

The rock is always a difficult place to land, even in summer. When the winter gales howled across its bleak expanse and the mountainous waves swept over it from one end to the other, it was sometimes impossible for weeks on end. Sam Burgess learned this to his sorrow when, one day in January, 1856, he set out in an open sailboat for Rockland, twenty-five miles away, in order to get food for the family and feed for the chickens. He left fourteen-year-old Abby, the oldest girl, in charge of the lights, her invalid mother, and her three little sisters. No sooner had he gone than the wind swung around into the northeast, and before long a gale was blowing which got worse as the days passed. Giant waves swept over the island carrying away an old wooden house and some smaller outbuildings. Fortunately, Abby was able to round up the chickens and shut them in the kitchen just before the chicken coop blew away, and now the plucky little girl had, in addition to an ailing mother, three frightened children, two lights, and a house full of chickens to take care of. But somehow she managed it, even though, as the days and weeks passed, she began to suffer from hunger and exhaustion.

Finally the storm blew itself out, and four weeks after he had left the rock, Sam Burgess was able to return to his post and his heroic little daughter.

It would seem that, after such a frightening experience, Abby would have wanted to move as far as possible from lighthouses. On the contrary, she grew up and married a lighthouse keeper, Isaac Grant, and they continued taking care of the lights together until the day she died. She spent forty years of her life in the lighthouse service, and when she died they buried her in a cemetery not far from the light she had tended for so long. Even in death, Abby did not want to be separated from her beloved lighthouses, and in accordance with her last wishes, her grateful neighbors placed a miniature light tower at the head of her grave.

Monhegan

Christopher Columbus is supposed to have discovered America in 1492. At least that's what we used to hear. If it is true, then Monhegan, a small rocky island only one and one-half miles long and one mile wide, just nine miles from Port Clyde off the coast of Maine, must be somewhere other than in America. There are any number of legends, dating back as far as the fifth century, mentioning this little island off the New England coast. It seems that not only the Norsemen, but the Welsh, Irish, and Latin sailors too, cruised in these waters hundreds of years before Columbus was born. Later on, in the 1600's, it was visited by a number of explorers we have all heard of, men like Samuel de Champlain, Bartholomew Gosnold, and Captain John Smith, the man who played such an important part in settling Jamestown, Virginia. Champlain called the island *La Nef* because he thought that from a distance it looked like a boat, and Smith referred to it as "a high round isle." Monhegan does look much like a boat, its low stern on the mainland side rising to the bow, a high rocky cliff on the

ocean side. And with the long Atlantic rollers breaking against it, the illusion of a ship breasting the ocean waves is remarkable.

Monhegan is a fishing community for the most part, except for a period of eight weeks in the summer when the islanders turn their attention to a more profitable business, tourism. During July and August people come from all over the country to admire Monhegan's rugged beauty, paint pictures of its lighthouse, and relax in its atmosphere of peace and quiet. Monhegan Island is twenty miles west of Matinicus in the direction of the Portland Lightship lying another forty miles to the westward. The much-painted lighthouse stands on top of a hill, showing up against the sky like the mast of a ship, adding greatly to the boatlike feeling. It has a white 170,000 candle power beam which flashes every thirty seconds.

Portland Head

The early settlers in this country had been too busy establishing themselves on land and setting up their new government to worry much about erecting lighthouses. But George Washington took a keen interest in maritime affairs, and shortly after he became President several lighthouses were built.

Our next beacon, Maine's first and best known lighthouse, was one of these. It was built on the mainland in 1787 at the top of Portland Head, Cape Elizabeth, near the entrance to Portland harbor. It is a beautiful spot, and every year thousands of people from all parts of the United States and Canada visit it to admire the view and take pictures of the tall white tower in its setting of blue sky, rocks, and foaming surf.

But no one was there to take pictures on Christmas Eve, 1886, when the skipper of the *Annie C. Maguire*, blinded by a driving snowstorm, had the bad luck to crash his vessel on the rocks almost on top of the lighthouse. He was lucky in a way, for this

made it easy to rescue all those on board. A line was quickly
made fast from the ship's mast to the base of the lighthouse, a
bosun's chair attached, and all hands hauled ashore safely, including the captain's wife clutching a hatbox containing all the family
money and jewels. The *Annie C.* was a total loss, battered to
pieces in a day or two by the pounding of the waves.

On another winter's night back in 1864, the liner *Bohemian*,
with 218 Irish immigrants and a crew of 95 aboard, was groping
her way through a heavy fog when she crashed head-on into Alden
Rock some distance offshore. She tore a big hole in her bottom
and the sea rushed in. There was no panic; the captain ordered
everyone into the boats and, one by one, they were loaded and
dropped safely over the side, all but one — the number 2 boat
turned turtle as it was being lowered, and the 50 men and women
passengers it contained were all drowned.

One of the lucky ones that day was a boy named John F. Fitz-
gerald, who probably will be remembered best for two things:
he was later elected mayor of Boston, and one of his grandsons,
John F. Kennedy, became the thirty-fifth President of the United
States.

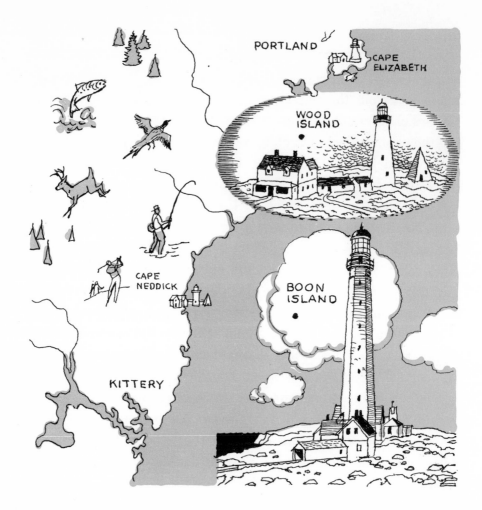

Wood Island

Continuing on our way down the coast toward Boston, we turn rather sharply southwest to Wood Island, at the entrance to Saco Bay, about twelve miles below the Portland Lightship. The lighthouse there was built in 1808 and rebuilt in 1858, fifty years later. The area around Saco Bay, like most of the Maine coast, has seen a great many wrecks and drownings. Well over a hundred vessels have probably been lost in these waters. Perhaps the worst disaster occurred in March, 1947, when three ships, caught in a great gale, went to the bottom within a few hours of each other.

The crews of two of them were lost, but the men on the third were luckier. Their vessel had broken in half, and the half carrying the crew grounded on some rocks near Cape Elizabeth. It broke up there, but only after it had held together long enough for the men to be brought safely to shore by breeches buoy.

It all sounds rather forbidding, but there were some amusing happenings at Wood Island too. Like so many of the lighthouses in these foggy waters, before the diaphone horn came along, Wood Island had a fog bell. At one point it also had a dog named Sailor, who had been taught to ring the bell by pulling the cord attached to the clapper with his teeth. Whenever he heard a ship's bell or whistle, he would run to the cord, grab it with his teeth, and pull with all his might. The dog was famous throughout Maine, and people would cruise miles out of their way in order to pass Wood Island and hear Sailor ring the bell.

Boon Island

We have pretty well covered the Maine lighthouses now. The next one is only nine miles from Kittery at the border of Maine and New Hampshire. Boon Island Light and its neighbor on Cape Neddick mark the end of the famous coast of Maine. There was no light on Boon Island when a vessel skippered by Captain John Deare was wrecked on the island. The crew got ashore all right, but week after week went by, and no one came near the place. There they were, with no way to leave, and no food. Eventually the situation reached such an extreme that the men drew lots to see which one would sacrifice his life to feed the others. Just how many survived this terrible ordeal of cannibalism is not known but it must have haunted them for the rest of their lives. Boon Island acquired its first lighthouse in 1791, and in 1852 it was replaced by a higher octagonal tower of granite, 137 feet tall.

Boon Island is another of those bleak, barren places with no trees or vegetation to soften the forbidding landscape. The water in the area is frequently so rough that it is impossible to land on the island. Such was the case in 1890. Beginning in late October there had been a series of bad storms, driving rains, and strong winds that had kept the lighthouse crew marooned for so long that provisions were running low. Toward the end of November the larder was almost empty, and it looked like a sad Thanksgiving with no turkey dinner. The night before Thanksgiving the storm, howling outside, was even worse than usual, and the rain was torrential. It was too much even for ducks, at least for the eight who, blinded by the light and swept along by the fierce gale, crashed headlong into the tower and fell lifeless to the rocks beneath. The next morning the lighthouse crew gathered them in and all hands dined royally.

On another occasion, when the bad weather had lasted for weeks, food in a barrel was floated to the men at the light, the wind and the tide carrying the cask of provisions to the hungry crew.

DOWN THE ATLANTIC SEABOARD

THE NEW HAMPSHIRE shore is as short as the Maine coast is long,
It can't be more than twenty miles from one end to the other. It,
too, is somewhat rocky but several big wide beaches help to make
it considerably less dangerous. Its most important light is the
White Island Light at the Isles of Shoals. Originally built in 1821,
it was rebuilt in 1859. Its 60,000 candle power beam flashing
every fifteen seconds is one of two lights that guide vessels into
Portsmouth Harbor, the other is Portsmouth Harbor Light right
at the entrance.

Not far below Portsmouth, Cape Ann, the second largest of the
Massachusetts capes, juts out into the ocean with the Gulf of
Maine on one side and Massachusetts Bay on the other. At the
end is the picturesque fishing village of Rockport, a favorite haunt
of artists who have a special fondness for boats and the waterfront.
In fact, there is one old wharf and fish house there that has been
the subject of so many paintings that it is known to artists all over
the country as Motif Number 1. Cape Ann Light, at the tip of the
cape, is just a stone's throw away on a small island offshore, while
just around the corner at the entrance to Massachusetts Bay, the
flashing red and white beacon of Eastern Point Light helps point
the way to Boston, where the Colonists erected their country's
very first lighthouse.

Boston Shows the Way

At the time Boston Light was built in 1716, there were only
seventy lighthouses in all the world and not a single one in our

part of it. The early settlers kindled a bonfire on a hilltop over-looking Boston Harbor back in 1675, but it was almost half a century later before they put up the first real lighthouse on Little Brewster Island in the harbor. It had a tragic initiation when George Worthylake, the first keeper, his wife and daughter, and George Saunders, who took his place, were all drowned within a year. This inspired young Benjamin Franklin, then only thirteen, to write a mournful ballad, "The Lighthouse Tragedy," which he sold with some success on the streets of Boston for a penny a copy.

Boston Harbor is often foggy and John Hayes, the next keeper, had a bright idea: He asked the city fathers for, and received, a cannon which he fired at intervals whenever the fog rolled in. This was the world's first fog warning signal, and for 132 years it boomed out until, in 1851, a huge bell was installed. This in turn gave way to a siren which today blasts out twice in rapid succession, once every minute.

Bad luck continued to follow the light. Lightning struck it once, and several times it caught on fire. But the greatest damage was done during the Revolutionary War when the British occupied Boston. Twice, a party of American patriots landed on the island and put the light out of commission, and twice the British repaired it. When they left in 1776, however, they also left a slow-burning fuse attached to a keg of gunpowder. They did their job so effec-tively that for seven years Boston was without a light at the entrance to its harbor.

Then in 1783 the present light was built on the ruins of the old. It was a massive tower of rubble stone and granite, eighty-nine feet tall with walls eight feet thick at the base. Like most light-houses, this historic tower is no stranger to storm, shipwreck, and sudden death. This one, however, has been around longer and witnessed more thrilling and terrible sights. There was the night the big square-rigger *The Montana*, driven by a blinding snow-

storm, piled up on the rocks near the light. She broke up quickly and most of her people were drowned. A few lucky ones managed to cling to bits of wreckage and reach the rocks, from which they were rescued, more dead than alive, the next day. On another night some fifty years later, the schooner *Calvin T. Baker* was blown on the rocks and held fast there. All night long the cries for help sounded across the water, slowly getting weaker, and all night long anxious rescuers waited and prayed for the wind to let up so they could launch a boat. But it was not to be, and the next morning three men, silent at last, were found frozen in the rigging.

The British were back off the coast of Boston during the War of 1812, and the lighthouse keeper and his wife watched helplessly while a naval battle was fought in which the American warship *Chesapeake* was forced to surrender after her captain had been killed and the heavier guns of the British frigate *Shannon* had reduced the ship to an aimlessly drifting hulk. The gallant Captain James Lawrence was spared the agony of surrender when he died on the deck of the *Chesapeake* whispering hoarsely, "Don't give up the ship," just nine minutes before she was forced to haul down her colors.

Minot's: The Killer Reef

Minot's Ledge, lying almost completely submerged in the ocean eighteen miles east, southeast of Boston, has always been a fearsome place. In the days before the white man came to New England, the Indians who lived along the coast stood in awe of the Evil Spirit Hobomock who, they were convinced, lived beneath the rocks from where he let loose the violent storms that so often battered the coast. From time to time, at low tide and in calm weather, they would paddle out to offer sacrifices of beads, dishes, or ornaments to appease the Wicked One.

The early settlers had good reason to fear the reef, too, for although they didn't believe in Hobomock, they had seen many a fine vessel go to its doom on the jagged rocks. In 1695 Anthony Collamore crashed his schooner on the ledge with the loss of all hands, and every year the toll of ships and lives increased. A vessel belonging to George Minot, one of Boston's leading citizens, was wrecked there in 1754, and from then on the reef was known as Minot's Ledge.

By 1847 so many ships had gone down and so many lives had been lost that the government sent an engineer, Capt. W. H. Swift, to the area to see what he could do. His solution was an iron skeleton tower supported by nine eight-inch wrought iron bars. Drilling the holes in the wave-washed rock was terribly dangerous work but, while they were drilling, the men were all roped to stanchions in the rock and no one was drowned, although several were injured by the battering waves. During the summer of 1848 workers were able to get the iron pilings in place; the following year, the living quarters and lantern room were added; and on January 1, 1850, the lantern was lit for the first time. The finished tower was seventy-five feet high with living quarters halfway up, supposedly out of reach of the waves. But they weren't, and the raging northeast rollers continually smashed against the wooden dwelling, hurling tons of water in the air far above the lantern room on its very top. Nine months of this was all the first keeper could take, and after several severe storms which had rocked the tower badly, Isaac Dunham quit and his place was taken by a man named Bennett and his two assistants, Joseph Antoine and Joseph Wilson. Bennett laughed at Dunham and called him a sissy. But one or two northeasters helped him change his mind, and he wrote to the authorities asking for an inspection of the light. They refused to help and, in March of that year, a hurricane struck, shaking the tower unmercifully. Though the structure stood up under the pounding, Bennett had had enough. He went ashore with the next relief boat and stayed there. It was a lucky thing he did, for the next day an even greater storm hit. Four days later it was still raging, rattling, and shaking the tower like a terrier with a bone and, by midnight of the sixteenth of April, Wilson and Antoine had given up all hope of surviving. They thought only of keeping the light burning as long as possible. Wilson wrote a message, "The beacon can not last any longer. She is shaking a good three feet each way as I write, God bless you all." He placed it in a bottle and threw it into the sea. Several days later it was picked up by a Gloucester fisherman. Unfortunately Wilson had been right, for sometime in the early morning hours the iron supports had snapped one by one, and the tower had buckled and slowly toppled over, carrying the two keepers with it as it sank beneath the waves.

A lightship was quickly moored nearby and Captain Barton G. Alexander of the U.S. Topographical Engineers began work on a

new lighthouse of interlocking granite blocks patterned after the famous one at Eddystone. For two seasons Captain Alexander worked at clearing the wreckage of the old light and putting up the framework of the new one. Then during the second winter, a bark named the *New Empire* was wrecked on the rocks and the work of two years was smashed to pieces. There was nothing to do but start all over again. This time, after three seasons of work, it was finished, six thousand tons of granite supporting a great bronze lantern almost one hundred feet in the air. But despite this great height, mountainous storm seas crashing against the tower's granite sides will, very often, bury the lantern in clouds of flying foam.

All lighthouses have a host of stories and legends surrounding them and Minot's has more than most, but the tales most often told are the ones about strange happenings and ghostly doings which no one can explain. For example, according to local legend the spirits of Joe Antoine and Joe Wilson have never left the spot. Perhaps not, for when one keeper went to clean his lantern, he found that, even though no human hands had been near it, instead of being tarnished and dull, the lantern was shiny and sparkling like new. And the local sailors all swear that before a storm the figure of Joe Antoine can be seen clutching the bottom of the

First tower   Second tower

ladder which leads from the surface of the sea to a doorway half-way up the tower, calling out a warning, "Keep away!" There have been unexplained tappings like those used by the early keepers to signal each other. Then, too, there was the keeper who fretted so much because there were no corners in the round rooms that he finally quit. One lonely soul complained he had "too much time to think." According to legend he solved the problem by cutting his throat.

Minot's Ledge Light is automatic now and there will be no more romantic tales growing up around it; but the beacon is still there, undaunted by the howling gales and battering waves, warning mariners to keep away from the murderous rocks of the country's most dangerous reef.

The Wicked Men of Scrabbletown

Cape Cod, where the New England coastline makes a right-angled turn toward the west, is a low-lying land of rolling dunes, sandy beaches, scrub oak, and pine. It is the summer playground of millions, and a portion of its Atlantic shore is now part of the National Seashore. In the early 1800's, though, the populace was concerned with grimmer business, the business of wrecking, for in those days the good folk of the Cape thought nothing of looting disabled vessels. Most people considered a wrecked ship and its cargo a gift from Heaven. And if Heaven seemed a little slow in providing these windfalls, they took matters into their own hands, luring passing vessels to their doom by means of false lights, called Judas lanterns.

The trick was to find a spot on land behind a reef, then, from the shelter of a dune, to wave a light attached to a broom handle gently to and fro so that the unsuspecting vessel would think it was the riding light of a ship at anchor and head for it, only to pile up on the reef. Then the fun would begin. The helpless vessel would be boarded and its cargo removed. If the captain and crew made no effort to stop this thievery, they were usually landed safely on shore. But if anyone objected, he got hit on the head with a brick wrapped in a sock. This weapon was commonly called a scrabble.

The people of Chatham must have overdone this practice somewhat, for the town was more often referred to as Scrabbletown.

Of course, this whole business worked only on dark and stormy nights when there was no moon; on nights when the moon shone brightly the bands of wreckers sat around biting their nails and cussing, which is why they were called moon cussers.

Practically everyone took part in this little game, and as a result, lighthouses were not very popular on the Cape. In fact, as late as 1839 when Nauset Light was built at Eastham, the local citizens were still protesting that it would take away their livelihood. Fortunately though, the Cape residents have found an even more profitable way of making a living; tourists by the hundreds and thousands, along with the motels, hotels, gift shops, and restaurants needed to cater to their wants, spell prosperity for the erstwhile "wicked men of Scrabbletown."

Nantucket

When Bartholomew Gosnold, the English explorer who made many voyages up and down the New England coast in the 1600's, first visited the long, narrow piece of land curling around Massachusetts Bay from the south and east, he named it Cape Cod in honor of the fish that he found there in such great numbers. It was well named for the early Cape Codders made most of their living catching and selling the lowly cod.

Oddly enough, Cape Cod not only has a fishy name, it looks like a fish hook, a bent and battered fish hook but still a fish hook, with Provincetown at the eastern tip acting as the barb on its end. The town of Woods Hole is at the opposite end, on the west, and beyond that, seeming almost to be part of the Cape itself, are the Elizabeth Islands. Farther out to sea lie the two larger islands of Martha's Vineyard and Nantucket. About fifty miles or so southeast of Nantucket the most famous old seamark in the North Atlantic, the Nantucket Lightship, flashes her warning.

As they near these shores, skippers of vessels making the North Atlantic run from Europe to the United States keep a sharp watch for this old lady, for not only does she issue a warning to "keep your distance," she marks the beginning of the last leg of their journey, a straight run of about two hundred miles northwest to the port of New York. The rest of the way is very well lighted. First, in case the navigator should veer a little to the north, there is Montauk Light on the eastern tip of Long Island to go by, followed some seventy-five miles farther on by Fire Island Light, and after that he will find the Ambrose Light Station and the Sandy Hook lights pointing the way directly into the harbor's lower bay.

Montauk

After the American Revolution, Montauk was one of the first lighthouses to be built by the brand-new government. President George Washington himself ordered its construction in 1789. The stone for the tower was quarried in New Hampshire and, in the winter of 1790, dragged by sled to Connecticut where it was loaded on barges and ferried across Long Island Sound to Montauk Point. There was some delay in getting started and the beacon took four years to build so that it wasn't until 1796 that the light actually functioned. When completed, though, it was as solid as a rock, with walls 8 feet thick at the base, so that it will prob-

ably last forever, unless the sea, which has been gnawing away at the cliff beneath it at an alarming rate, finally reaches the tower and tumbles it into the sea. The water has already moved from a distance of 345 feet to within 50 feet of the lighthouse. At that rate, the end will come about the year 2000, unless something is done to stop the erosion. Montauk Light is an 8-sided tower, 168 feet high, with a 200,000 candle power white flashing light, radio beacon, and fog horn. The tower is white with a broad red stripe running around the middle. It is a beautiful structure and the $2400 John McComb was paid for designing it seems hardly enough, even though money went a lot further in those days.

There was danger, for a time, that the lighthouse would be torn down by the Coast Guard to make room for an automated loran tower. It would have been, too, had not the state of New York come to its rescue by naming the old lighthouse to the National Register of Historic Properties, which means that as a federally owned historic site, it is safe, at least for a while.

Fire Island Light

Continuing on his way to New York, our transatlantic skipper next looks for the flashing white beam of the lighthouse at Fire Island Inlet which marks the entrance to Great South Bay, about seventy-five miles east of Montauk. There used to be a major lighthouse at Shinnecock Inlet, about halfway between Montauk and the Fire Island Light, but it was abandoned in 1948 and replaced by a secondary light, a completely automated steel skeleton tower with a red flashing light, fog horn, and radio beacon.

Fire Island has one of our most important lighthouses. Not only is it the first light a great many navigators see when they arrive here from Europe, but it is almost the last, for it is only about thirty-seven miles to Ambrose Light Station and the Sandy Hook lights at the entrance to New York Harbor.

When it was originally built in 1827, the Fire Island Light was only 74 feet high, too low to be seen from any distance, and, as a result, there were several wrecks in the area. One ship, the *New Era,* had been loaded to the gunwales with hundreds of adventuresome immigrants. When she went down in 1854, she took 300 persons, hopefully looking for a place to live in the United States, with her. Two years later work was begun on a new tower off the Fire Island Inlet, this one to be 167 feet tall, more than twice the height of the old one. It was finished in 1858 and, after that, navigators had no trouble seeing the Fire Island Light, though they sometimes mistook it for the Sandy Hook Light which is a little farther to the west. The new tower was certainly a great improvement over the earlier one but it did not put a stop to further sinkings. In 1884 a 900-ton British ship, the *Charles Hickman,* loaded with cannel coal and empty petroleum barrels, ran aground off the inlet. It was a cold stormy night, a night of pelting rain and pounding surf, and it wasn't long before both the fore- and mainmasts collapsed to the deck in a tangle of wreckage. Then the bow broke off, leaving the crew huddled together in the slowly sinking stern. One of the men of the nearby Forge River Life Saving Station who was patrolling the beach, saw the floundering hulk and summoned the crew of the station. Despite the almost impossible weather, they were able to rig a breeches buoy and, one by one, the men were hauled to safety.

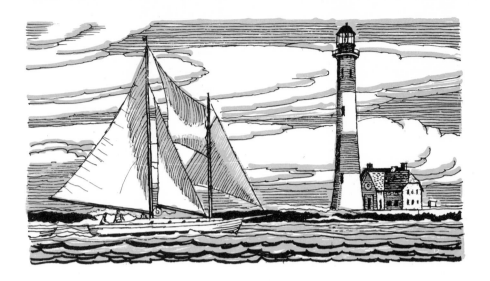

Some of the crew arrived more dead than alive, for the waves were so high that the trip ashore was more like an underwater swim than a ride in a breeches buoy. However, the men all came through, and the only person to lose his life was a boy who drowned when he and a companion tried to make the trip together. One of the boys succeeded and the other almost did. The breeches buoy carrying the two was only a few feet from the beach, and a Coast Guardsman, up to his armpits in the boiling surf, had hold of one boy when suddenly, the other half-drowned boy was snatched from his arms by a big breaker and swept away into the night.

There have been other wrecks along this section of the coast but nothing to compare with the numbers at places like Minot's Ledge and Cape Hatteras. In fact, most people are not even conscious of any danger in these waters. They think of Fire Island as a place to sail, surf, swim, and sun.

The light itself contributes considerably to this holiday atmosphere; the tall graceful tower, boldly painted in four black and white horizontal stripes, and the neat white buildings and fences suggest a giant toy, left there by a forgetful child from Gulliver's land of giants.

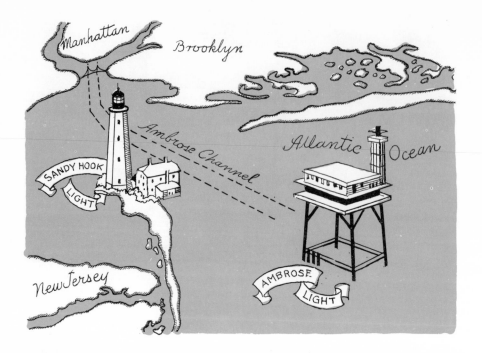

Ambrose

Ambrose Light Station lies in the open sea about ten miles equidistant from Rockaway Point, New York, and Sandy Hook, New Jersey. A ship approaching New York from either the south or the east can't miss it. A course from Ambrose Light heading northwest and aimed halfway between these two points will lead a vessel up the middle of Ambrose Channel, through the Lower Bay to the Narrows and through this entrance to the Upper Bay to the docks on the Hudson and East rivers.

The early citizens of New York recognized the importance of this spot and, even though there already was a lighthouse on shore nearby, they put a lightship, the *Sandy Hook,* here way back in 1823. Because it marked the entrance to the newly dredged Ambrose Channel, eighty years later its name was changed, and though the actual vessel was replaced from time to time, there was an Ambrose Lightship stationed there until 1967. In that year the last of the ships was taken away and a huge ocean data and light station, made of concrete and supported by steel piles driven deep into the ocean's bottom, was placed there instead. Meanwhile, there are two more lights that we must pass before we enter the Lower Bay and they are both on Sandy Hook.

Sandy Hook

This narrow sandy strip of land, five miles long, extends north from the Jersey shore, pointing like a slightly curved finger toward Staten Island and New York City. A fingernail was added to the finger when, in 1764, a lighthouse was built. The money for it was raised by selling chances on a large cash prize. At least some of it was, for the sum collected in the lottery fell short of the amount needed, and the rest was raised by a tax on the tonnage of vessels passing the lighthouse. The completed tower, made of stone, was 103 feet high and octagonal in shape, tapering from a width of 29 feet at the bottom to 15 feet at the top. The lantern, a huge affair, 7 feet high and 33 feet in circumference, held 48 separate oil blazes whose light was combined by means of a number of mirrors and lenses into a single beam.

It had only been up about twelve years when the Revolutionary War broke out and the British occupied New York. The Americans, grabbing at the chance to make things difficult for the enemy, lost no time in sending a raiding party ashore under cover of night to dismantle the light. They did a good job but the British quickly repaired it, whereupon the Americans came back and put it out of commission again. Again the British repaired the light. It wasn't attacked again, the British were driven out of New York, and Sandy Hook Light is still there. Although it isn't a major beacon anymore, it is the oldest original lighthouse still in service in the United States of America. To be entirely truthful, it isn't quite all the original tower; it was renovated in 1817, and some new building material was added, but basically it is the same.

Today, vessels heading for the Lower Bay place their main reliance on a skeleton steel tower at the very tip of the hook, Sandy Hook Point Light. It has a more powerful automatic light, a six-second equal-interval vertical beam, which can be much more easily seen and identified than the old landmark.

The Statue of Liberty

The list of famous lighthouses is long, and the list of tales about them even longer; these are stories of disaster, storm, and wreck, tales of faith and hope, too, and of the men and women who tended the lamps, and their courage and unswerving devotion to duty. So it seems odd that the most famous lighthouse of them all, the one beacon known to more people than any other in the whole world, is one that has known no wrecks; it is the subject of no colorful legends; and it is not even listed in the Coast Guard's list of lights — odd, that is, until you realize that the light's name is Liberty Enlightening the World or, as she is more widely known, the Statue of Liberty.

This colossal copper figure of a woman, the largest statue ever made, was given to the United States by France in 1884 as a token of friendship between the two countries and to commemorate the French and American revolutions. The standing figure, clad in a flowing gown, holds a blazing torch in her upraised right arm and clasps a tablet bearing the date of the Declaration of Independence close to her body in the crook of her left arm. She wears a crown like a burst of sun's rays upon her head, and a chain, symbol of oppressed people everywhere, lies broken at her feet. The Statue of Liberty stands on a granite pedestal above the star-shaped remains of old Fort Wood on Liberty Island (formerly Bedloe's Island) in New York's' Upper Bay; her welcoming light shines out 305 feet above the waters of the busy port where millions of immi-

grants, eagerly looking forward to life in the New World, and countless returning travelers, happy to be back home again, have seen her and have felt their hearts skip a beat at the sight.

Every year, thousands of visitors take the one-mile boat ride from Manhattan's Battery Park in order to pay their respects to the old girl. Inside the statue many climb the 161 steps of the narrow, spiral staircase which leads to the head; others just stroll around, enjoying the view and the sea air.

Cape Henry and Cape Charles

Farther down the coast, in Virginia, two capes face each other across the entrance to Chesapeake Bay. On April 26, 1607, a party of thirty people, led by the distinguished English explorer Bartholomew Gosnold, who had named Cape Cod and, along with Captain John Smith, helped establish the nearby Jamestown settlement a year earlier, landed on the more southerly of the two. They named the place Cape Henry and set up a large cross on a high bluff overlooking the ocean to commemorate the event. The Jamestown settlement did not turn out very well. Most of the early settlers either tired of the hard life and went home or fell ill and died. Nevertheless, over the years the Colony of Virginia prospered greatly, due in no small measure to the many excellent rivers and harbors in the area and the consequent steady growth of the maritime trade. And Cape Henry and Cape Charles, its neighbor to the north, were destined to play a large part in that growth.

Back in 1718 when Alexander Spotswood was governor of Virginia, a group of North Carolina planters called at the executive mansion one day to ask him to do something about the notorious pirate Edward Teach. Teach, better known as Blackbeard, had been cruising the Caribbean and the coastal waters, looting and sinking ships, and killing people right and left for several years. Of late, he had been using North Carolina as a base of operation and some people even went so far as to say that he and the governor were in cahoots and that the governor shared in the pirate's ill-gotten gains.

Hearing this, Governor Spotswood wasted no time in hunting Blackbeard. Two navy sloops with orders to bring Blackbeard back dead or alive were immediately dispatched to find the pirate ship. Teach had become so bold that he made no attempt to hide. One of the sloops, commanded by Lieutenant Maynard, was lucky enough to locate the pirate ship a few days later, and in the fight that followed, she was boarded and Blackbeard was shot and killed.

With this black-hearted scoundrel out of the way, the coastal trade picked up and the shipping interests began to press for better lighting of the harbors and coastal waters. That same year (1718) another delegation called on the governor, this time to plead for a lighthouse to be built on Cape Henry to mark the entrance to the bay. Governor Spotswood was agreeable but the British Board of Trade, which had the final word in maritime matters, refused the project. And the people of Maryland, who certainly could have been expected to be for it since the bay was largely in their state, didn't seem to want it either. Alderman Perry was of the opinion that it "would be useless in a fog and not needed in clear weather," and the idea was postponed indefinitely. Spotswood never was able to do anything about the lighthouse project; and Governor Gooch, who followed him in office, made several abortive attempts to whip up interest in it without much luck, until 1773 when the assembly met and finally voted to appropriate money for a lighthouse on Cape Henry. Once the money was available, matters moved along rapidly, a site was selected, and work was started on the light almost immediately. It ended just as abruptly when the rock to be used in the tower, ferried in small boats for one hundred miles and then unloaded directly on the beach, was completely buried by tons of sand washed up by storm-driven waters.

At this point, war broke out between the Colonists and their English rulers and it put a stop to any further attempts to build the tower. As soon as the war had been won and the new government had become accustomed to its responsibilities, Congress took up the matter of the Cape Henry Lighthouse again, and early in 1791, they chose John McComb to build it.

McComb, who was then a young man in his early thirties, must have been highly regarded as a lighthouse engineer, for just one year earlier he had been picked by President George Washington to build one at Montauk Point. He was already at work on this project when he accepted the Cape Henry job. He was also responsible for the Cape May Lighthouse in New Jersey and the first New York City Hall — a very busy young man indeed.

The Cape Henry Lighthouse, an eight-sided tower made of sandstone, was completed in 1792. It was still standing in 1861 when the Civil War began, but it was so severely damaged in the early days of the fighting that it was out of commission for over a year. During this period, when the light was out, a lightship was anchored just outside the bay to mark the entrance. In 1866 the lighthouse was again in need of repair. The old wooden staircase had become too rickety and had to be taken out, and a circular iron staircase was installed in its place.

By this time, though, the sandstone tower was showing signs of collapse; great cracks were showing up in its sides, and everyone agreed that a new (and taller) light was needed. They also agreed that iron was a more suitable building material than sandstone, and so the new lighthouse was to be made of that metal.

It was begun in 1880, but disaster struck almost immediately. In order to bring the iron to the site of the tower, the engineers had to construct a 4-mile tramway ending in a wooden pier capable of supporting the freight cars and the iron. This was a heavy load

to bear, and before long, the marine boring worm, which lives in the sea and is very fond of his diet of wood, had so weakened the wooden supports that one freight car fell through the pier. Though most of the iron was removed from the pier before the whole thing collapsed, it was a very narrow escape. From then on everything went along smoothly and the 170-foot tower was completed some time in 1881.

Its 170 feet made it the tallest fully enclosed iron tower in the country. The lighthouse is striking looking, with a wide black band around both top and bottom. The area in between is divided in half horizontally with wide vertical black and white stripes, creating a checkerboard pattern overall. It flashes a white 160,000 candle power beam with a red 50,000 candle power glare to mark the nearby shoals. Cape Henry is not as dangerous a spot as Cape Hatteras, farther to the south, but the seas can still be very rough, and many ships have been lost within sight of the lighthouse. During World War II, this section of the coast became a favorite hunting ground of German submarines, and by the time the war was over, at least a dozen vessels had been either torpedoed or sunk near the light by gunfire from these prowling wolves of the sea.

It seemed certain, back in 1872, that the old lighthouse was about to fall down; after all she was eighty years old and coming apart at the seams. She didn't though, and as the years went by it became increasingly clear that she wasn't going to. Eighty more years passed and then some and it seems now that, under the careful supervision of the Association for the Preservation of Virginia Antiquities, the old girl could live forever.

Across the water to the northeast, a piece of land shaped like a lobster's claw reaches out toward Cape Henry as if to close the entrance to Chesapeake Bay. This is Cape Charles. In 1828, thirty years after the lighthouse had been erected on Cape Henry, a light was built on the easternmost tip of Cape Charles in order to mark more clearly the entrance to the bay. Fifty-eight years later it was still there but so damaged by erosion that it had to be rebuilt. The reconstructed tower did not stand up very well and a few years later, shortly after the outbreak of the Civil War, work was begun on a new tower. Construction continued satisfactorily until the beacon had reached a height of eighty feet, or a little more than half its projected height. At this point, a band of guerilla fighters attacked the tower and partially destroyed it, putting an end to the project for the moment.

It was finally completed, under very heavy guard, in 1864. All this time the sea had been making great inroads on the land around the lighthouse, and the tower itself was rapidly deteriorating. In 1885, it was decided to build a new one, and in order to protect it from the encroaching waters, a number of jetties were constructed around the structure while it was being built. Although the idea seemed a good one, it didn't work; one rousing northeaster was all that was needed to wash away large sections of jetty so that the work had to be abandoned.

Congress, after taking a close look at the project, decided that it would cost too much to continue it and that the site was too near the ocean, anyway. Originally the beacon had been 600 feet away

1827

1895

from the shoreline, but the greedy waters had eaten away more than half the land and now it was less than 300 feet from the water's edge. The legislators postponed the whole idea indefinitely and nothing further was done until 1895. By this time, the pressure on the government for a new lighthouse was too strong to resist, and Congress voted funds for a new and taller tower. It was to be an iron cylinder tower, 191 feet high, surrounded and braced by an octagonal pyramidal skeleton structure. And, of great importance, the site chosen was three quarters of a mile inland, well out of reach of the ever-advancing ocean. This was a wise precaution for the site of the first tower is now underwater and the encroaching sea is slowly but steadily creeping up on the tower built in 1864.

Mariners used to complain that the Cape Henry and Cape Charles lights were so much alike that they couldn't tell one from the other. No doubt it was confusing. In any case, the new Cape Charles Lighthouse was given a much more powerful beam than the Cape Henry light, 700,000 candle power, so that no one need wonder which one is Henry and which is Charles.

The Graveyard of the Atlantic: Cape Hatteras Light

In 1905, when the Wright brothers were looking for a suitable place to try out their flying machine they finally settled on Kill Devil Hill, one of the highest dunes on the beach at Kitty Hawk, North Carolina. Except for the gulls, who must have looked on in wonder as the big yellow bird with the strange wings hopped into the air, they had the place to themselves. And since the sand gave them a soft landing place for their flimsy biplane, it was truly an ideal test spot. But for vessels headed north or south past Cape Hatteras, it was a different story. This outer barrier of wind-swept sand dunes is probably the most dangerous part of our whole coast. It is called the Graveyard of the Atlantic and rightly so, for although there are no rocks to smash a ship's hull, the violent storms, shallow water, and drifting sands are even more deadly. The first wreck recorded there was in 1526, and since then over two thousand ships have been lost in these waters, including the ironclad *Monitor*, which survived the Civil War, only to capsize and sink during a hurricane off the Carolina cape. It even looks like a graveyard, for here and there among the dunes the rotting timbers and rusty fragments of long-forgotten wrecks stick up above the sand and clumps of waving beach grass as if to mark their graves. Towering over this lonely scene is the tallest of all our lighthouses, the 208-foot black and white candy-striped Cape Hatteras Light. It wasn't always that tall. The original tower, built in 1789, was only 90 feet high. But this wasn't high enough to be seen from the ships

at sea. Twice, another lighthouse was begun offshore on Diamond Shoals, but each time the sea washed it away and the project was finally given up.

The present tower was built in 1871, and though it was placed some distance back from the water's edge it, too, was almost destroyed by the sea. Over the years the pounding waters gnawed away at the dunes, creeping closer and closer to the lighthouse until, in 1938, it was lapping around the base, and the tower had to be abandoned. The light was moved to an iron skeleton tower farther inland, and in one last effort to save it, a number of barriers were erected around the base of the old lighthouse. Slowly the dunes re-formed; the sea was forced to retreat, and in 1942 the towering light was once more standing guard over the Graveyard of the Atlantic.

Death on the Tower: The Story of Cape Florida Light

Thanks to the bands of Indians, pirates, and wreckers who, for more than one hundred years, had claimed it as their own, the beaches of Key Biscayne in southern Florida had grown accustomed to scenes of violence and bloodshed long before Cape Florida Light was built in 1826. It had been the stamping ground of the notorious pirate Black Caesar, who terrified the coast for many years until he was finally caught and hanged in 1718. So it came as no surprise when one fine day in July, some ten years after it was built, the Cape Florida Light was the scene of a desperate and gallant battle against overwhelming odds. The keeper and his family had gone to town to shop early that morning, leaving Assistant Keeper Thompson and Henry, an old handyman, in charge. While they were gone a band of Indians attacked the tower. Thompson and Henry barricaded themselves inside, but the attacking Indians set fire to the doors, windows, and the tanks of oil. To escape the flames, both men retreated to the top of the tower,

carrying muskets and a keg of powder. They cut away the stairs directly beneath them and fought as best they could from the iron balcony while the flames crackled all around and the air was filled with flying glass from the broken lantern. Henry was killed in the fierce exchange of bullets and Thompson, who had been shot in the foot while fighting below, was wounded again. With his clothes on fire, and in danger of roasting to death, he summoned all his remaining strength and, in a last desperate effort, heaved the keg of gunpowder into the flames below. The explosion that followed shook the tower, but it blew down what was left of the burning staircase. The heat was less intense now and Thompson, half unconscious on the balcony, was able to endure it. The Indians, thinking him dead, left after first burning down the keeper's house.

Fortunately, the blast had been heard some miles offshore by the captain of a naval vessel who came quickly to investigate, only to be faced with the problem of helping the wounded Mr. Thompson down from the balcony nearly eighty feet above the ground. He managed to get a line to the top of the tower by using his musket to fire twine which the wounded man caught. Then a tail block was hauled up, two men were hoisted from below, and Thompson was lowered to safety. The lighthouse was fired on again during the Civil War when it was shelled by gunboats. Later, it was put back in service and was used until 1928, when the Fowey Rocks Light was built several miles offshore. Today, Cape Florida Light stands peacefully in the newly created state park. And now, groups of happy bathers, skin divers, and picnickers, instead of the colorful desperados of old, have taken possession of its surrounding golden sands.

UP AND DOWN THE PACIFIC COAST

THERE IS SOME TRUTH to the words of a popular song of the 1920's which pokes fun at joining the Navy "to see the world," for "the Atlantic isn't terrific and the Pacific isn't what it's cracked up to be." This is true at least as far as the Pacific is concerned, for Pacific means peaceful, and this vast body of water, the largest and deepest of all the oceans, is often far from that. As a matter of fact, Pacific storms are something special. The powerful currents, terrific winds, and sheer weight of the great mass of water all help to produce some tremendous disturbances. In addition, tidal waves, the result of subterranean upheavals deep under the ocean floor, sometimes come crashing in on the Pacific shores killing great numbers of people and wiping out in an instant what man has taken many years to build. In 1946 one such wave, rolling in from the direction of China halfway across the world, swept up a cliff in Alaska, completely destroying a lighthouse perched there far above the surface of the sea, and retreated carrying the bodies of all five crew members with it.

Pacific fog, like that of the Maine coast, is thick and impenetrable. And there is a good deal of it, so much so that the first lighthouse built in southern California at the entrance to San Diego Harbor had to be abandoned because its beam was often blotted out by a high fog.

The shoreline itself is quite different from that of the eastern seaboard. The Atlantic coastline, except for the very northern section, is low, with sandy beaches slipping gently into the sea, so that in order to be seen from the water, the lighthouses themselves have to be tall. In the West, however, the sites are so high above the sea that the lighthouses themselves can be much smaller. In fact one exists that is only twenty-five feet high. Then, too, there are not nearly so many obstructions in Pacific waters as there are in the Atlantic: fewer rocks, reefs, and ledges, and the shoreline is not nearly so broken up by rivers, inlets, and bays. As a result, the Pacific coast has fewer lighthouses and they are naturally farther apart, except in areas where they are needed to guide vessels into major ports like San Diego or San Francisco.

San Francisco is California's largest bay, and today, the city itself is one of the world's greatest and busiest ports. Yet in 1848, when gold was discovered in Sutter's Creek in California, there were only 800 people in the entire city. One year later the population had increased to 25,000 and they kept coming until it seemed as though everyone was after the legendary gold.

San Francisco was headquarters for it all, and great numbers of ships carrying cargos of necessities and luxuries, pickaxes and perfumes, sledgehammers and toothpicks, everything under the sun that anyone might need or want, headed for San Francisco hoping to acquire a share of this "gold mine" of people itching to spend their new-found wealth. Too many of the ships never made it, ending up on the rocks and submerged reefs that weren't even marked on the charts. The resultant loud howl of anguish from ship owners, businessmen, and others whose pocketbooks were suffering was finally heard in Washington, and in 1855 the government built lighthouses on both the Farallon Rocks and Point Bonita.

The Farallon Rocks and Point Bonita

The Farallon Rocks, some of them barely showing above the waters, lie twenty-three miles west of San Francisco's Golden Gate.

As islands go, they are quite ordinary; some are small, some large, but all are equally dangerous to shipping. About all they are good for is to provide resting places for the great numbers of seals, sea gulls, and sea lions who, from time immemorial, have had the place to themselves.

The largest of the islands rises steeply above the water, and it is there they put Farallon Light. It was a difficult spot to build on, as the workmen had to carry the building materials a brick or two at a time up the face of an almost perpendicular cliff. It was slow work, and when they had finally finished the lighthouse proper and began working on the lantern and lens, they found that the light was too big to fit in the tower. So they tore the whole thing down and started over again.

This time there were no obstacles, and Farallon Light was completed and went into service in 1855. The seals, sea gulls, and sea lions who had left the scene while work was going on have all returned and have taken up business once again, seemingly undisturbed by the strange creature with the raucous voice and flashing eye who sits on top of their biggest rock.

Point Bonita Light, built the same year as Farallon, stands on, or rather hugs, the top of a one hundred-foot cliff just outside the Golden Gate. It squats low on the rocky headland, so low as to seem almost like a part of the natural rock formation. The tower is on the outermost point jutting far out into the sea, and in order to reach it, visitors must cross a small suspension bridge slung over a deep gap in the rock's surface. It was here that the West Coast's first fog cannon was used, fired by Sergeant Pat Maloney who was supposed to shoot it off every half hour "when the fog was in." This was fine in clear weather, but poor Pat soon found out that "when the fog was in" meant most of the time, and after a siege of three days and three nights of cannon firing with only two hours sleep, he quit. Others must have felt the same way, for in 1857, just two years after the first shot was fired, the cannon was silenced forever and a hand-operated fog bell took over the fog warning job.

Point Montara and Alcatraz

Point Montara Light, just across the bay from Bonita, and the San Francisco Lightship, stationed outside the bay in 1898, were a great help to the vessels approaching the harbor. But once past these two, only one beacon stood inside the fifty-mile-long bay to light the way. This was Alcatraz Light, California's first lighthouse, erected in 1854 close against the great gray fortress of Alcatraz prison, its lantern raised high above the massive walls as if to keep watchful eye on the men locked inside.

Alcatraz, familiarly known to criminals everywhere as "the Rock," was built on an island in the bay by the Spaniards, who were the first to settle here. Originally a fort, it was for some time a military jail. In 1933 it was turned into a maximum security prison for civilians: a place where only the most desperate criminals were sent; for no one, it was thought, could possibly escape from the Rock. Ever since 1937 there has been some doubt about this, because in that year, two men managed, by crawling through drain pipes and ventilators, and dropping from a small window to the rocks below, to reach the water and disappear into the fog. They probably were drowned in the icy waters, but since no bodies were found, no one can be sure. In any event, no one tried again until 1958 when two others, after tying up a guard, entered the water; one got no farther than a group of rocks near shore, and the other's body was found floating face down in the bay five days later. In June of 1962 three more men disappeared from the Rock leaving no trace except a waterproof plastic bag containing some small personal effects found floating not far from shore. The only other attempt came six months later. Two men, Scott and Parker, with the aid of makeshift water wings made out of inflated surgeon's rubber gloves and the sleeves of prison shirts, escaped. But one got cold feet; he became so cold all over, in fact, that he turned back before getting very far. The other, Scott, made it to shore but passed out from exposure and exhaustion as soon as he got there and was picked up and returned to finish his sentence. So you see, although perhaps not impossible, escaping from the Rock is really pretty difficult. Prisons, though, like almost everything else, grow old and outlive their usefulness. Repairs and maintenance at Alcatraz became so expensive that in 1963 the government moved the inmates elsewhere and abandoned the prison, leaving the island to a caretaker and his wife, the gulls, and the wild flowers that bloom in profusion around the crumbling walls of the once-dreaded Rock.

Mile Rocks

Out in the middle of San Francisco's harbor, but only about one-half mile from shore, despite their name, lie two rocks known as Mile Rocks. The largest of the two, a ledge about forty feet by forty feet, lying with its top just barely covered by the waves at high tide, has a lighthouse on it now. But it had none in 1901 when the liner *Rio de Janeiro,* proceeding confidently on her way to port, crashed into it, ripping a great hole in her bottom. She sank like a stone, taking 115 people along with her to their deaths. Mile Rocks Light, like a headstone on a watery grave, marks the spot where she went down. The original structure was a round tower, the lower half a solid concrete cylinder resting on the ledge and supporting three other sections, each one stepped back from the one below, with a large lantern atop all so that the tower looked something like a partly opened telescope standing on its broad end or a five-tiered wedding cake waiting to be cut.

Whoever made the light a bachelor station knew what he was doing, for the only way to get ashore is to climb down a swaying, twisting, twenty- or thirty-foot rope ladder hanging from one of two catwalks that extend from opposite sides of the tower to get into a small boat bouncing around on the waves underneath. One of these catwalks is used at high water and the other when the

Mile Rocks Light before the two top sections were removed

tide is out. On returning to the light, clutching and grabbing for the elusive ladder while doing a balancing act in the boat isn't much fun even for the hardiest coastguardsman, and it is practically impossible for a woman.

In 1966 a submarine power cable almost two miles long connecting the lighthouse with the mainland was completed. With this new source of power a lighthouse keeper was no longer needed and Mile Rocks Light became completely automatic. At the same time the lantern and the two top sections were removed, and, though it still shows a light and sounds a fog warning, the remaining lower half of the lighthouse is a sad-looking piece of architecture.

Point Arena

Some distance up the coast, on another of California's rocky cliffs, lies Point Arena Light, the second of the two towers built there. The first one, erected in 1870, was destroyed in 1906 by what everyone but San Franciscans refer to as the San Francisco Earthquake. The people of San Francisco, who would rather forget the earthquake part, speak of it as the "Big Fire." Call it what you will, the result was the same — the lighthouse was destroyed, and in an effort to foil both 'quake and fire or any other of Mother Nature's little tricks, the new one was built of reinforced concrete, making it the first such lighthouse in the country.

Pigeon Point

I suppose fog has been the cause of more shipwrecks than any other single thing, especially before the days of the radio beacon. It certainly spelled doom for the clipper ship *Carrier Pigeon*. On

the night of June 6, 1853, she was groping her way up the California coast toward San Francisco in a dense fog. She was about fifty miles short of her destination when she ran aground off what was then known as Whale Point. It was calm when the *Pigeon* hit, and the crew all got safely ashore suffering only a little wetting in the process. The next day a violent storm developed, and the vessel and her valuable cargo were pounded so fiercely that nothing but her figurehead, a beautifully carved and gilded pigeon, was salvaged.

The local people couldn't forget the night when the lovely clipper, fast aground, fluttered like a great white bird in her agony to escape, and they renamed the point Pigeon Point. There were many more wrecks in the same area, and finally, some eighteen years later, Pigeon Point was given a lighthouse, a tall brick tower boasting a 450,000 candle power beam and a nine-foot revolving lens. The lens, taken from Fort Sumter Light in South Carolina at the outbreak of the Civil War, had been buried in the sand of Charleston beach in order to keep it from being destroyed in the fighting. It stayed there, unharmed, all during the war years until, in 1872, it was dug up and shipped to Pigeon Point where it was installed in the tower and was found to work perfectly. Pigeon Point in the old whaling days was a grim spot; hard work and tragedy were the order of the day. But over the years the picture has changed, and now partly because of its natural beauty and its position on State Route 1, the people from nearby Santa Cruz, along with artists, and tourists from the East, have turned it into a recreation spot, so that today Pigeon Point is probably California's most popular lighthouse.

Point Arguello

Far to the south, just below Point Honda, whose rocky shores are strewn with the bones of wrecked vessels, Point Arguello Light shines out brightly, pointing the way to the Santa Barbara Channel and the port of San Diego. This is foggy, foggy country. In 1923 Arguello was one of the first lighthouses to have a radio beacon. Unfortunately, to some skippers at that early date, the radio beacon was just a new, untried gimmick and they preferred to navigate by dead reckoning, a term which sometimes described what happened all too accurately. For instance, although it was foggy one particular December night in 1923, Captain Edward Watson, in command of a squadron of seven destroyers headed for San Diego, either did not hear or chose to ignore the radio signal. He turned his flagship sharply toward land about fifteen miles before he should have and ran head on into the rocky shore. All six vessels, following the leader in close formation at high speed, piled up behind him on the wicked rocks. Twenty-two sailors died that night in the chain reaction and the seven vessels were a total loss. Point Arguello Light, first established in 1901, was rebuilt in 1934 and the light is even brighter now, sweeping the skies with the power of 1,100,000 candles.

St. George's Reef

At the other end of the coastline, up near the Oregon border, California's most northerly lighthouse, St. George's Reef Light, stands in lonely splendor on Northern Seal Rock. No one even knew that this rock was out in the ocean six miles from the nearest land until one July day in 1865. Captain Sam deWolfe, resplendent in his captain's uniform and gold braid, and secure in the belief that he was in safe waters, was calmly pacing the bridge of the Pacific liner *Brother Jonathan* as she steamed proudly along at full speed. Her bow wave was curling sharply away from either side; as seafaring men would put it, "she had a bone in her teeth" and her wake spread wide behind her. The passengers were amusing themselves on deck or in her saloons when, without warning, the ship hit something with a great crash. The impact tore her bottom out and she sank almost immediately, dragging down the 200 passengers to their deaths. It was a great tragedy, and unfortunately this is how lighthouses get to be built. In due course, one was begun on St. George's Reef of Seal Rock in 1882. As was true so often before, it was tough going; the workmen had to be quartered on a schooner close to the site and landed and taken off

in a cagelike structure strung on a cable running from ship to reef, while the huge precut granite blocks, each weighing several tons, had to be slung in rope nets, lifted gently ashore, and there carefully fitted together. It was risky work but no one was drowned, even though once in a while someone slipped off the reef and got an unexpected soaking. The schooner was blown off station several times, the work was held up at one point for lack of funds, and what with one thing and another the lighthouse was not finished until 1891. It is a white square tower on an irregular oval concrete base about 80 feet long and 50 feet high, faced with granite. The light itself is 146 feet above the water. It also turned out to be the most expensive lighthouse this country had ever built, costing about $750,000, and one of the loneliest; for the weather here, when it puts its mind to it, can be perfectly dreadful. Sometimes for weeks on end it is impossible to land on the rock and just as impossible to leave it. There was one spell of 59 days when the men in the light were completely shut off from any communication with the mainland. They were actually in danger of starving to death. Their tempers grew shorter and shorter until finally they reached a point where their nerves were so frazzled that they couldn't even speak to each other. Eventually, however, the sun came out, the wind stopped howling, the waves subsided, relief came from shore, and for a short time at least St. George's Reef Light was back to normal.

The Rock of Tillamook

Any ocean lighthouse is a lonely place. Standing in the open sea, surrounded by forbidding rocks and powerful currents, its only visitors are apt to be the gulls and terns who can come by air, or an occasional seal sunning itself on the rocks. But some lights are more lonely than others. The Coast Guard says the four loneliest — and most dangerous — ones are Mt. Desert, Matinicus, Minot's Ledge, and Tillamook. The first three are fairly close together off the New England coast, the fourth is three thousand miles away in the Pacific Ocean, nineteen miles south of the mouth of Oregon's Columbia River. The words *lonely* and *dangerous* describe it perfectly, for although it is only one mile from the nearest land, it is almost as difficult to get ashore at Tillamook as to land on the moon. It took one party seven weeks before they finally made it.

One side of this huge rock rises 200 feet almost straight up from the bottom of the sea to the surface and continues on another 71 feet to the summit. From there it slopes gradually to the water's edge on the other side. Here, during a storm, the long rollers rush up the slope to break in a wild burst of flying foam over the top.

It was just about a hundred years ago — the West was booming;

whaling, lumbering, and increasing trade with Hawaii meant more ships sailing the seas, and more ships on the rocks. A lighthouse was desperately needed on Tillamook, but even though the government had provided the money, construction was more easily talked about than done. In the first place, a road twenty miles long had to be built in order to bring supplies to the nearest jumping-off place on the mainland.

Getting ashore on Tillamook was an even harder job. One man was drowned before Charles Ballantyne, the engineer in charge, and nine others managed to land safely, bringing with them a few tools and supplies, including dynamite, to use in leveling off the top of the rock.

Leaving Tillamook was just as difficult as getting there. The men could travel back and forth from the supply ship by means of a bosun's chair hung on a cable running from the ship's mast to the rock, but it was usually a wet, uncomfortable ride. Once on the rock the men were glad to stay put. After building a shelter part way down the sloping side, they set up a derrick below it on a ledge, so that in calm weather supplies could be landed directly from the deck of the supply ship. Then the task of building the tower began in earnest.

It was dangerous work and no day passed without someone getting a ducking, but luckily no lives were lost and the stone dwelling with its high tower in the middle was completed in February, 1881, less than two years after the first dynamite blast. It was quick work, but it was not in time to save the lives of the twenty souls aboard the English bark *Lupata*, which had brushed by Tillamook in a heavy fog four weeks earlier only to be wrecked later on the Oregon shore. It passed by unseen but close enough for the men on the rock to catch the faint sound of voices coming from the doomed vessel. Fog is bad enough, but when the mountainous Pacific waves, driven by one hundred mile an hour winds, hurl themselves against the great rock, it is truly a terrifying sight. Time and again the lantern high above the sea has been broken by flying stones churned up from the bottom of the ocean, and once during a storm a huge boulder, hoisted aloft by a giant wave, came crashing through the roof of the keeper's dwelling. Another time, the station's three 730-gallon tanks, full of water, were tossed around like pebbles by the angry seas and left piled in a heap against a corner of the building. The telephone cable resting on the ocean's bottom has been broken and the fog horn silenced, its throat choked with sea water and stones.

Wind and waves have battered this lonely outpost for more than three quarters of a century but, despite the frequent damage, Tillamook Light, like the rock on which it stands, has proved it is there to stay.

Cape Flattery

Cape Disappointment and Cape Flattery

Washington's Cape Disappointment, jutting out into the ocean on the north side of the Columbia River, was given that name by the skipper of the ship *Felice* in 1778 because he had tried to find the entrance to the river and couldn't. Others, attempting the same thing, were caught on the sandy shoal which stretches a greedy hand from the river's mouth far out into the ocean. A light was sorely needed here, but it was not until seventy-eight years later that Cape Disappointment Light was built. A year later another major beacon, Cape Flattery Light, was erected on an island at the entrance to the Straits of Juan de Fuca which separate Vancouver, British Columbia, from the United States. This rounds out the list of major outer beacons stretching from southern California to the Canadian border. Then there is a gap before the lights begin again in Alaska.

LIGHTS IN ALASKA

"SEWARD'S FOLLY" they called it, or sometimes "Seward's Icebox," when William H. Seward, who was our secretary of state at the time, bought Alaska from the Russians in 1867. He paid $7,200,000 for it, and at first glance the price did seem a little high, for this huge hunk of real estate, over one-half million acres so far away in the arctic regions, was pretty much of a mystery: a vast, cold, primeval wilderness inhabited only by wild animals and a few natives called Eskimos, who lived in little ice huts and ate polar-bear meat and seal blubber. At least that was the popular idea. But the ocean was full of riches: whales, seals, salmon, and other fish; the forests sheltered great numbers of fur-bearing animals such as bear, fox, mink, and otter; the ground held untold riches of copper and gold; and it wasn't long before Mr. Seward began to look less and less foolish, particularly as more and more people kept moving into the territory.

The seafaring men were the first to come, the whalers and seal hunters and salmon fishermen. They came to fill the holds of their ships from this seemingly inexhaustible supply. On land, the trappers, too, were getting rich, but the real rush to Alaska came when gold was discovered — first in California in 1848 and later the big Alaskan strikes in Juneau, the Klondike, Nome, and Fairbanks. People soon found out that Alaska, especially the southeastern part bordered by the Pacific Ocean and protected from it by a chain of outer islands, was perfectly livable country. It had short, hot summers and long, cold winters, but good soil suitable for growing things, with plenty of fish in the streams and game in the forests. A good many people liked what they saw and decided to settle there. All this activity brought more and more vessels moving up and down the coast — and more and more wrecks on the rocks and reefs all along this rugged, treacherous shoreline. And no wonder, for there wasn't a single lighthouse in all this vast region until 1902. Two were built that year, the first of many secondary lights, mostly along the Inland Passage in the southeastern part of the territory.

This protected waterway offered a comparatively safe route along that section of the coast which is known as the Panhandle. It is a narrow strip of land over five hundred miles long and varying in width from a few miles to more than a hundred, lying between the Gulf of Alaska on the west and the Canadian province of British Columbia on the east. However, the journey to Anchorage, Kodiak, and on through the Bering Sea to Nome in the far north is a longer, tougher trip, twenty-five hundred miles of open sea, so it is along this route that Alaska's half-dozen major lighthouses were erected.

Cape Decision and Cape Spencer

Cape Decision is on the Alaskan shore, about a hundred and fifty miles above Cape Muzon, Alaska's most southerly point, and as the name suggests, offers the skipper headed up or down the coast a choice of routes: on one side the sheltered waters of the Inland Passage and on the other the open sea. If he is headed north on the outside route, the next light he sees will be Cape Spencer, another hundred and fifty miles toward the northwest. There is a good chance, however, that he won't actually see it, for the fog around the entrance to Cross Sound sometimes blots out the light completely. But fog or no fog, there is always the radio beacon and the hoarse roar of the diaphone horn to guide him on his way.

Cape St. Elias Light

Cape St. Elias and Cape Hinchinbrook

Next in line, if all goes well, will be Cape St. Elias with its one million candle power beam, the most powerful of the Alaskan lights. This is followed about two hundred miles farther on by Cape Hinchinbrook Light, on Hinchinbrook Island. When a light was first put here in 1910, it stood on the edge of a cliff overlooking the sea where it stayed for more than twenty years. Then, for some unknown reason, the cliff started to crumble away carrying the lighthouse with it. Huge cracks began to appear in the side and the keeper had to leave in a hurry. Needless to say, when a new one was built, it was placed far back, away from the dangerous area.

Scotch Cap and Sarichef

Take a look at a map of Alaska. See if you don't think it looks like the head of an elephant with its trunk lifted and pointing in the direction of Russia. To get to northern Alaska by water, a ship must go around the uplifted end of the trunk into the icy waters of the Bering Sea and there, at the very tip, on barren Unimak Island stand two of the loneliest lighthouses in all the world: Scotch Cap and Sarichef Lights. Scotch Cap lies on the south shore, and Sarichef is seventeen miles away on the other side of the island.

The forbidding shores of this bleak island are blanketed by fog most of the time and battered constantly by the pounding surf whipped up by the savage gales roaring in from the far reaches of the Arctic Ocean. It's lonely all right, sometimes a whole year will pass when no one can either land on or leave this desolate shore. Several times, in emergencies, when food has been low or there has been a sick man at the light, attempts to put a boat ashore have ended in failure, and in one instance six lives were lost when the rescue boat capsized in the angry surf. No wonder

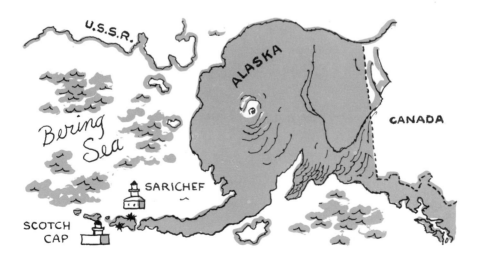

the men who tended these lights were allowed six months on shore for each year at the light. It was a step in the right direction, but it probably should have been the other way around. These lonely outposts are the lights that vessels traveling back and forth between the Orient and our great Northwest depend on, and hardship or no hardship, until they are made completely automatic, men will have to go on risking their lives to tend them.

Tragedy at Scotch Cap

One disastrous incident occurred about 1:30 on the morning of April 1, 1946. The man on duty in the radio shack high up on a cliff at Unimak Island, where the Pacific Ocean meets the icy waters of the Bering Sea, was going about his business as usual, checking his instruments and occasionally glancing out the window, where the blackness of the night was regularly interrupted by the flaming rays of Scotch Cap Light which stood about thirty feet below, part way up the cliff.

It was a bleak and lonely place and the radio operator leaned back in his chair and let his thoughts carry him homeward, far away from the harsh realities of life on Unimak. But he came back with a jolt as the building suddenly shook violently, the doors and windows rattled, loose objects were sent flying, and lights flickered off and then on again. Then all was quiet.

Earthquakes are common at Unimak so the man did not give it much thought. Some time later, however, a second and stronger shock occurred, and after putting things which had been shaken loose back in their proper places, he checked by radio phone with the man on duty at the light, who was a little shaken up but reported no great damage.

This should have been the end, for earth shocks usually came in twos and the officer in charge at the radio shack, who had been peacefully sleeping until routed out of his bunk by the force of

the shocks, was reassuring the man on watch, when with a roar that sounded like a thousand jet planes, a great wall of water burst against the cliff, pounding up the sides, filling the air with debris and flying spray, and stretching greedy fingers toward the radio shack at the top. As quickly as it came, it went, leaving a hush behind it. Outside in the pitch dark, the night was empty, no flashing light, no fog warning, no buildings to show where the light had been, and the officer in charge, after ordering his men to higher ground, turned to his transmitter and sadly broadcast the bad news of the tidal wave. He talked by telephone with the men at Sarichef on the other side of the island and waited impatiently for daylight. With the first faint flush of dawn the shocked radio men picked their way through the tangled mass of rubble which was all that was left of the lighthouse station, finding no signs of life, no clothing, and no bodies except for one small piece of what might have been an arm or a leg.

The quakes continued for several weeks and about a week later several bodies were found floating in the sea, but there was no new tidal wave.

When a new light was built, it was put higher up on the cliff where it is thought to be safe from any more attempts by Nature at an April Fool prank.

PACIFIC OUTPOSTS

TWENTY-TWO HUNDRED miles directly south of Unimak, out in the
middle of the Pacific Ocean, lies a little group of about twenty
coral-fringed volcanic islands discovered by Captain James Cook
in 1778. He named them the Sandwich Islands in honor of his
friend the Earl of Sandwich, the same man who achieved immor-
tality by putting a piece of meat between two slices of bread.
The natives called the largest island Hawaii, and since neither the
islanders nor the Americans who came later cared much for the
name given them by Captain Cook, the whole group came to be
known as the Hawaiian Islands. It became a protectorate of the
United States in 1900 and our fiftieth state in 1959.

Hawaii

No cold, no snow, no icy winds, and believe it or not, no fog mar
the delightful climate here. Lofty mountains, wide sandy beaches,
exotic flowers, luxuriant foliage, brilliantly colored birds, trade
winds gently blowing through the waving palms — people come
from the four corners of the earth to enjoy these natural pleasures
and to relax in this lovely little corner of paradise. Relaxing was
nothing new here; the natives had been doing it for generations.
And except for a little fighting among themselves to keep the
population within bounds, and a little fishing to keep the rest of

them alive, they continued to do it; although after Captain Cook brought the islands to the attention of the white man, the pace began to accelerate a bit. The whalers were the first to come, a hard-drinking, ungodly lot, followed by large numbers of missionaries bent on saving souls. Other people came to work the soil, raising sugar, rice, coffee, and a few pineapples but, by and large, things went on just about the same way they always had until, in 1900, Hawaii was made a protectorate of the United States. Then things began to happen with a vengeance, all kinds of things: huge sugar and pineapple plantations were developed, high-powered publicity campaigns were organized, hula dancers, tourists, surfers, luxury hotels — and lighthouses — began to appear. But it was the airplane that caused Hawaii's greatest boom, for the Pacific Ocean is very big and the great metal birds that carry passengers and freight up and down and back and forth across this tremendous body of water welcome a chance to land on these islands, rest awhile, and refuel before taking off again for wherever it is they are going. And wherever it is, one thing is certain: when they get there it won't be half as lovely as the little group of islands way out in the middle of the Pacific Ocean.

There are only five islands of any size in the group: Hawaii, the largest; Maui; Molokai; Oahu, perhaps the best known; and Kauai. Two of the smaller ones, however, are noteworthy: Lanai was a former prison camp for women and later became known for its huge pineapple plantations, and Kahoolawe, now just one great mass of volcanic rock, was once a prison camp for men only. After the Americans took over, the Air Force used Kahoolawe as a practice target and the ground is covered with unexploded ammunition, bombs, shells, and grenades, so that it is dangerous to walk anywhere on the island. The men who tend the one light on the island stick close to a cleared path that leads down from the landing place to the light. Even the birds sit down gently when they land on Kahoolawe, for fear of hatching an explosion.

KILAUEA POINT

LEHUA ROCK

Kauai

Niihau

Oahu

N

W

S

BARBER'S POINT

MAKAPUU POINT

PEARL HARBOR

HONOLULU

MOLOKAI LIGHT

Molokai

PAUWELA POINT

Lanai

Maui

Kahoolawe

Hawaii

CAPE KUMUKAHI

Lighthouses of
HAWAII

Cape Kumukahi Light

Cape Kumukahi is one of about six big lights in the Hawaiian Islands. It stands on the most easterly point of Hawaii where its powerful 1,700,000 candle power light flashes a welcoming message to travelers from South America. Kilauea Point Light at the western end of the group on the island of Kauai is only a little less powerful, and it marks the end of the road for ships and planes coming from the Orient.

Most people shudder at the thought of leprosy; they think of lepers as unclean and leprosy as being highly contagious. Consequently, when a leper colony was established in 1860 on Molokai Island, everyone stayed as far away as possible, everyone, that is, except Father Damien, a Belgian missionary priest who went there to live and help and remained to die — of leprosy. Even the gentlemen back in Washington, halfway across the world, when asked for money to build a light on Makaualua Point, next door to the leper colony, shied away at first. They eventually did allocate the money, though, and the light built there in 1909, Molokai Light, is the most powerful (2,500,000 candle power) in the islands. This is the one the navigators look for when approaching Hawaii from Canada and the states on the mainland.

Molokai Light

When most people speak of Hawaii, they are really thinking of Oahu. Everyone has read about or seen pictures of the city of Honolulu and the beautiful beach at Waikiki where golden brown bathers, gathered here from everywhere under the sun, ride the long Pacific rollers. Diamond Head is here, too, the much-photographed extinct volcano that guards the entrance to the harbor. And last but not least are the great naval, air force, and marine bases on the island: Pearl Harbor, Hickam Field, and Wheeler Field. It was the surprise bombing of these bases by the Japanese on the morning of December 7, 1941, that pushed the United States into World War II. On this, the blackest day in United States naval history, 200 Japanese planes struck so suddenly that only 6 out of 126 planes on the ground at Wheeler Field managed to get into the air, and 83 were either destroyed or severely damaged. We lost 5 battleships (completely destroyed) with several others, along with some cruisers, put out of action. The loss in men was staggering — over 3000 killed or wounded. Truly a black day for the United States, for the Japanese lost fewer than 100 men, 5 midget subs, and only 29 planes. There is an old saying that "one swallow doesn't make a summer" and the jubilant Japanese soon found out that it takes more than one victory to win a war. On September 2, 1945, aboard the U.S.S. *Missouri,* the Japanese signed a formal surrender.

Back in 1870 when Honolulu was the home port of the Pacific whaling fleet, the whalers placed a lantern on top of the Customs House in the harbor, draped some red cheesecloth around it to make it easily identifiable, and Honolulu had its first lighthouse. The light is stronger now (200,000 candle power) but it is still there above the Customs House, the oldest light in the islands. Barber's Point Light on Oahu's southwest coast is by far the most powerful on that island; Makapuu Point Light on the northeast coast, while not so bright, is over four hundred feet above the water and can be seen from a distance of twenty-eight miles. Since there is no fog here, the higher the light the better; in fact there is a lighthouse on the island of Lehua which is probably the tallest in the world. Built on a towering mass of rock, its light is over seven hundred feet in the air.

There are many secondary lights around the islands but the only other big one is on Maui, the second largest of the islands, at Pauwela Point, commanding the entrance to Kahului Harbor.

Lehua Rock Light

Other Outposts

Now the line of outposts jumps a long way west across the Pacific to Midway Island, 1150 miles northwest of Honolulu. Midway was the scene of one of the decisive battles of the Second World War, when the flower of the Japanese air force went down to defeat and the Japanese navy was just about wiped out. Some 3400 miles directly to the west of Honolulu lies another of our remote Pacific outposts, the little island of Guam; while far to the south about halfway between Honolulu and Australia lies Samoa, where Robert Louis Stevenson, author of *Treasure Island*, *Kidnapped*, and *A Child's Garden of Verses*, lived and is buried. This rounds out our line of outer defenses.

Sarichef, Unimak, Molokai, Oahu, Guam, Samoa — strange names from far places, nevertheless as American as apple pie, and all part of the great system of Pacific outposts designed to keep our country safe in case of enemy attack.

WHERE ICE IS KING

THEY ARE RIGHTLY called the Great Lakes; no other name could do justice to their size and breathtaking beauty. Lake Superior, the largest, 350 miles long and 160 miles wide at its widest part, is the largest freshwater lake in the world. And two of the others are almost as big. On the map, this odd-shaped cluster of five lakes suggests a bursting Fourth of July rocket or perhaps an assortment of ragged bits of cloth hung out to dry and fluttering in the breeze. If you happened to find yourself on the deck of a ship afloat on any one of them, however, with no land in sight and a full gale ripping through the rigging, you would swear that you were out in the middle of the ocean during a particularly violent storm. For nine months of the year, this great inland waterway is a well-traveled highway alive with fleets of vessels loaded with grain, petroleum, coal, iron ore, and other products of this fabulously rich area. During the other three months, the icy blasts of winter roaring down from the North Pole across the frigid surface of Hudson's Bay keep gathering momentum as they come, until the full fury of their icy breath hits the waters of the lakes, turning the whole region into one vast deep freeze. Salt-water sailors are inclined to look down on their freshwater brethren as sissies or, at best, amateur sailors, but not if they have ever sailed the lakes, for these five sisters can unloose weather to match the dirtiest that the Atlantic or Pacific oceans can produce: fog, wind, rain, waves, blizzards, with something extra to boot; for unlike the oceans, which do not freeze over, the Great Lakes for a good part of the year turn into one huge cake of ice.

It begins in November when, without warning, the temperature will take a sudden drop one night, and before anyone realizes it there is a thin crust of ice on the water. All through November, while the ice builds up, the ice breakers keep pounding away at the ice pack trying to keep the channels open as long as possible.

By mid-December, though, the wind becomes more bitter, the mercury huddles in a little ball in the bottom of the thermometer, and the ice takes over completely. Navigation comes to a standstill, the freighters and tankers hole up in one or another of the few ports which stay open all year, and the ice breakers retire to their corners to take stock of their wounds and repair the damages in readiness for another crack at their archenemy, the ice.

Sometimes, though, Old Man Winter is too fast for the ships and the ice closes in on them before they can get away. Something like this happened one night in early December, 1937, when eight vessels were frozen in solid as they were trying to make port near where the Detroit River runs into Lake St. Clair. It took two powerful ice breakers and two Coast Guard cutters working day and night for three days to free them.

Lake Huron

The lighthouses in this wintry waste take a terrible beating from the ice, which not only piles up around them in great hunks that crunch and grind against them all winter, but covers them from top to bottom with an overcoat of frozen rain and spray. For this reason, the first thirty-four feet of Spectacle Reef Lighthouse in

Lake Huron were made of solid granite. And a good thing, too, for once when the keepers came to take over the light in the spring, they found the ice packed solid all around it for a half mile in all directions and piled up in huge blocks to a height of forty feet against the tower. They even had to cut away a large iceberg which had forced itself into the door. Once every year the lighthouse men who tend these giant popsicles play a dangerous game, gambling on how late they can stay on duty without getting trapped in their towers. It's like playing Russian roulette with ice instead of bullets. This takes pretty good nerves, but as far as I know, up to now they have all made it safely to shore.

During the open season, Spectacle Reef Light shows alternate red and white flashes of 35,000 and 45,000 candle power, but when winter finally settles in and everything is frozen up tight, a steady white beam of 110 candle power takes over, more, I imagine, as a gesture of defiance to Old Man Winter than for any good it might do.

Lake Superior

We know that ocean lighthouses are often placed far out at sea. Mt. Desert Light, for instance, is more than twenty miles from shore. But one would hardly expect to find a lighthouse in the middle of the North American continent, over a thousand miles from any ocean and even farther than Mt. Desert Light from the nearest land. Nevertheless, there a light stands in Lake Superior twenty-three miles from shore, surrounded by thousands of miles of fresh water and coastline. The shore is very much like the coast of Maine, with the same spruce forests and rugged beauty and just about as long. It is Stannard Rock Light, one of the most isolated lighthouses to be found anywhere in the world. The nearest port is forty miles away and, when the ice takes over, it might just as well be four hundred.

Whitefish Point, at the eastern end of Lake Superior, is the most dangerous spot in the lake. So many vessels have been wrecked here that it has earned a reputation like that of Cape Hatteras. They call it the Graveyard of the Lakes. The government took note of this danger early and built a light here in 1849. Whitefish Point Light was the first to be erected in Lake Superior and also by far the most powerful, with a 700,000 candle power beam, almost twice as bright as any of the others.

Lake Michigan

Lake Michigan runs from north to south, so that the arctic winds driving down from the Pole have swept, unhindered by any obstacle, across 307 miles of open water before they run smack into the skyscapers of Chicago at the southern end of the lake. No wonder Chicago is called the Windy City. Maybe someday, now that the St. Lawrence Seaway is completed, and vessels can bring their cargos all the way from Europe to the heartland of America, it will be the busiest as well as the windiest.

Lake Michigan's first lighthouse was erected here at the mouth of the Chicago River in 1832, the first of several which now stand guard over the port of Chicago. The brightest of these, at 140,000 candle power, is the Chicago Harbor Light.

Lake Michigan's winds were responsible for a near tragedy back in 1876 at the Michigan City Light, the most southerly of Lake Michigan's lighthouses. The tower was a wooden structure built on the keeper's dwelling. The keeper, eighty-year-old Mrs. Harriet Colfax, had been tending the light for many years. One night during a violent windstorm, she climbed the tower as usual to refill the lamp, even though it was shaking so violently that on the way she spilled most of the oil. She filled it as best she could and climbed down again. Seconds later there was a sudden burst of wind, and tower and light disappeared into the night.

Lake Erie

Lake Erie is not nearly so deep as the others, not much more than sixty feet at its deepest point, but its shallow waters are none the less dangerous. Very little wind can kick up very big storms here in the twinkling of an eye, some of which are so violent that vessels have been known to disappear completely, never to be seen again. In 1913 a lightship vanished from her station off the harbor of Buffalo at the height of one of these storms, and it was seven months before she was found, resting on the bottom of the lake more than a mile away from her post.

Lake Ontario

Although Ontario, the most easterly of the chain of lakes, is the smallest, she is still a very big body of water. And when she is in the mood, she can kick up a storm that even Lake Michigan would be proud of. Only one third of her shoreline belongs to the United States, which is fine with the Coast Guard as the Canadian government takes care of most of the aids to navigation. The biggest and oldest of Ontario's lighthouses is the one in Rochester Harbor built in 1822 with a 15,000 candle power light. The last of our lights on the lake is at Tibbetts Point, which juts out into Lake Ontario just where the St. Lawrence enters the Great Lake.

LIGHTHOUSES THAT GO TO SEA

EVER SINCE the days of the Roman galleys, ships have carried lanterns at their mastheads to prevent collision with other ships. Ships designed solely for the purpose of guiding and warning others are comparatively new in the annals of the sea. The first real light vessel was anchored in the mouth of the Thames River in England in 1773, several thousand years after the first lighthouse had been built. We in the United States didn't start our lightship program until 1820 with a lightship in the more or less sheltered waters of Chesapeake Bay. Three years later the first "outside" light, the Sandy Hook Lightship, took her station just outside New York Harbor.

The earliest lightships were simple affairs, something like a raft with a rounded deck like a whale's back to keep out the water and a stubby little mast supporting a lantern. They had no sail or crew, so someone had to visit them every day to light the lamps, or put them out, look for leaks, and check the moorings. They were miserable little vessels; the lights kept going out, and all too often they either capsized or broke loose from their moorings and drifted away. They were soon replaced by small wooden sailing vessels with crews of three or four men who lived aboard and took care of the light. By 1892 the wooden hulls had given way to iron, and steam had taken the place of sails. Then, in 1930, the first Diesel-electric powered vessels went into service.

This was a great advantage whenever the moorings broke, for with Diesel-electric power the ship could get underway almost immediately, while the steam engines had to waste precious time waiting for a head of steam to build up before they could start to move.

If *I* had to choose between a lighthouse and a lightship as a place to work, there isn't much doubt about the one I would pick for there are two things about lighthouses that are very comforting:

1) once you are in them, you always know exactly where you are;
2) as long as you stay there you will never suffer from sea-sickness.

There are other advantages too, such as better living quarters with more room to move around in, dishes and pots that stay put, and real beds that don't rock and roll. The lightship, on the other hand, floating on the surface of the sea, connected to solid ground only by its anchor chain, is never very stable; the quarters are cramped, and the bunks are just bunks. And if the wind blows hard enough for long enough you may end up somewhere other than where you think you are.

Sinkings are rare but they do happen occasionally. We mentioned that a lightship disappeared completely on Lake Erie during a violent storm, and in a hurricane in 1944, the light vessel stationed off Cuttyhunk in Vineyard Sound was sunk, leaving no trace except the two bodies which washed up on shore a few days later. Too often the lightships, unable to leave their stations, serve as targets for other vessels. Ships lost in the fog are apt to head directly for the sound of the horn and, despite the radio beacon and their own radar, get so close to the lightships before they realize it that they run right into the little vessels. The lightship anchored off Fire Island was hit in 1916, and in September, 1934, the liner *Olympic* on her way to New York crashed head on into the Nantucket light vessel and sank it. Ambrose Lightship, marking the channel into the port of New York, was run down and sunk by the freighter *Green Bay* in 1960. Thanks to Bobby Pierce, the boatswain's mate who gave the alarm in time, no one was drowned. More often, though, the light vessels are just blown off their stations by the hurricane winds, and they are able to battle back to their proper positions.

As recently as January, 1966, a howling winter storm tore the Ambrose Lightship loose from her moorings, driving her seven miles off station even though she was using her Diesel power to fight the force of the wind. Getting back on station against head winds and angry seas takes time and, meanwhile, there is no warning light at the danger spot. The lightship herself has to be dark, too, until she gets back, for a warning signal in the wrong place is far worse than no signal at all.

No bed of roses, these lighthouses that go to sea; nevertheless, they do the job when it is either too dangerous or just impossible to put up a regular lighthouse. At places like Minot's reef, for instance, when the first lighthouse built there in 1851 was destroyed less than a year later, it seemed foolish to try to build another one and a lightship was moored there instead. It was there for four years but by that time the lighthouse engineers had learned enough about the science of lighthouse building to try again, and the present tower on Minot's Ledge is the result.

Diamond Shoals

There are still a few places where wind, sea, and sand have conspired to foil all man's attempts to build a fixed-base lighthouse. Diamond Shoals, a group of sandbanks stretching ten miles out to sea from Cape Hatteras, is the best known.

Cape Hatteras Light, the tallest of our lighthouses, stands on the shore, and fourteen miles at sea, not far from the outer edge of the shoals, the Diamond Shoals Lightship is anchored. Her job is to see that passing vessels steer clear of the deadly area. Nine hundred feet of heavy iron chain attached to a 7800-pound mushroom-shaped anchor buried deep in the sandy bottom, hold her more or less securely in place. In the early days it was definitely "less securely," for the first lightship to be placed there was swept from her moorings so often that she spent more time away from the station than on it; and the second, which took its place three years later, was smashed to bits by the raging seas. At this point the engineers were a little discouraged. They decided to try buoys, but buoys were not the answer. One of them was picked up on the coast of Ireland about a year after it had disappeared from its place on the shoals, and a number of others just vanished. In 1884 a report on the buoys' success put it rather clearly. It said, "It is evident that such a buoy cannot be maintained at this point." Since neither lightship nor buoy had been successful, and not knowing what else to do, Congress, in 1889, hopefully authorized the building of a lighthouse on the shoals. This was easier said than done. The first attempt was washed away shortly after construction had gotten underway, and the second try, three years later, met the same fate. The government then decided to try once more to anchor a lightship on the deadly shoals. They placed one there in 1897, and except for the times that it has been carried away by storms, it has been there ever since. It takes a strong wind to move it; the 1938 hurricane dragged the ship 5 miles, and in 1967 the 150 mile an hour winds of a winter storm tore her loose from her moorings, but I think that was the last time the stout little lightship was forced off her station.

Usually after one of these big blows when the lightship had been dragged from her moorings, she found herself five or ten miles farther out to sea and able to get back on station without too much trouble. It happened often enough that the crew had learned to accept it as part of the day's work. On one occasion, though, they got more than they bargained for. It was at night during a particularly violent storm, when the winds were rampaging and the seas were running mountain high; a Japanese cargo ship, badly damaged by the storm, was taking on water and rolling helplessly in the trough of the waves nearby, and the little Diamond Shoals Lightship was pitching and straining at her anchor chain — but holding — until one gigantic wave, with the force of the whole Atlantic Ocean behind it, crashed head on into her bow. One of the anchor chain's massive links snapped, and the lightship was on her own, tossing like a cork on the angry seas. All seemed lost, when unbelievably, a following wave, what must have been the granddaddy of all waves, swept under her keel and, lifting the floundering vessel high in the air, carried her upright clear across the sandy shoals and deposited her high and dry on

the beach. There was no great damage — some broken dishes in the galley and a few broken bones among the men — and as soon as things had calmed down again, the crew dug a trench around the ship, a dredger was called to clear a channel through the sand to the ocean, and in no time at all the Diamond Shoals Lightship and her plucky crew were back in business.

It hasn't always been just the weather that caused trouble at Diamond Shoals. Human nature can be pretty ornery, too, like the time when the crew of one light vessel mutinied. The weather had something to do with it, for the men had been isolated in their floating home for over a month because of gale force winds and rough water, and their nerves were on edge. The mate and the engineer, in an effort to ease tension, joined the members of the crew in a game of cards. This, of course, was a breach of discipline: officers are not supposed to mingle socially with ordinary seamen, and the captain reprimanded his two officers severely for it. When they objected, he grew angry, drew a pistol, and threatened to put them in irons, whereupon the two officers disarmed the captain and locked him in his cabin. Later, when a relief ship arrived, he was released and he and the rest of the crew, all except the mate, went ashore. The police promptly arrested them all. The captain, who had only been trying to maintain discipline, and the crew, who were just fed up, were tried and convicted of desertion. The mate, as a reward for not leaving the ship, was promoted to captain.

A lightship is a peace-loving vessel whose job it is to protect property and save lives. One could hardly be expected to be involved in a naval action. Nevertheless, toward the end of World War I, one of ours was sunk by enemy gunfire. On August 6, 1918, a German submarine surfaced near the Diamond Shoals Lightship. She was after a heavily loaded little freighter, steaming quietly along on her way up the coast. The submarine didn't bother to fire a torpedo but used her deck gun instead to sink the unsuspecting cargo ship. The lightship had no armament, so she could not join in the fighting, but she did have a radio and the skipper literally filled the air with frantic warnings to all shipping to stay clear of the area. He had to be quick, for the Germans wasted no time in coming back and sinking the vessel. The U-boat commander spared the crew, however, and they all reached shore safely in their lifeboat. This was the only time a lightship was actually sunk by an enemy, although they sometimes took part in sea battles in other ways.

For some time before we entered World War II, German submarines had been operating off our coasts. On one particular day off the Nantucket area, in sight of the lightship, they had sunk ship after ship. By the end of the day the crews of six torpedoed vessels, 115 shipwrecked sailors, were housed in the Nantucket Lightship, while a string of fourteen lifeboats bobbed up and down at her stern like a mother duck with a brood of duck-lings. A year or two later, some time after we had entered the war, another lightship, this time on the West Coast off Blunt's Reef, was involved in a shooting incident. The crew of the lightship there stood helplessly by while a Japanese submarine torpedoed a freighter. This time, too, satisfied with having sunk the cargo vessel, the submarine slipped quietly away and the lightship crew picked up the shipwrecked sailors and landed them safely on shore.

Nantucket Lightship

Diamond Shoals is probably the more dangerous locality because of the very severe weather around Cape Hatteras, but Nantucket Lightship is undoubtedly the most famous of all the light vessels anchored off our shores. This is because of her position, marking an extensive shoal area fifty miles west of Nantucket Island and two hundred east of New York. She serves as the traffic officer of the main North Atlantic sea-lane to and from the European con-tinent. The sight of the little red vessel with the winking eye is as familiar to the skippers of the huge ocean liners that speed between New York and points abroad as a particular stoplight might be to you. Inbound ships heading for New York take their bearings on the ship as they hit the home stretch, while out-going vessels, on seeing the flashing 20,000 candle power beam or

the bright red hull, get squared away for the direct run across the Atlantic.

The first lightship to be stationed here dropped anchor about nineteen miles southeast of the shoals in 1854. Less than a year later, she broke loose and was driven ashore on Long Island near Montauk Point. She wasn't too badly damaged and, after being repaired, she was towed to a new station, three miles off Sandy Hook at the entrance to New York Harbor. They rechristened the lightship *Scotland* in memory of a liner, the *Scotland*, which had been wrecked at this spot. She stayed there seventy years. A new vessel, the famous *Number I*, took over the *Scotland*'s job at Nantucket in 1856. This one served thirty-seven years before it was moved. Like all the others, *Number I* broke loose every so often, twice during her last year on the shoals. She had no power and had to rely on sails to maneuver, so that each time she parted her moorings, she was forced to run before the wind to remain seaworthy. The first time she broke loose it was nine days before she could halt her headlong flight. The second time it was even longer, a full two weeks before she could start sailing back to her port.

Number I was the last of the old sailing lightships; from 1892 on, all the vessels were driven by steam or Diesel engine. With this new source of power, the vessels were better able to buck the stormy winds and stay on station during a blow. Despite these occasional breakaways and frequent close calls from vessels on a collision course, no one had lost his life at the Nantucket Lightship in all the eighty years since it was established, until one foggy spring morning in 1934.

No storm this time, the sea was like a millpond: no wind, no waves, nothing but fog, fog that settled over the sea and crept silently into every nook and cranny of the ship, hiding all its familiar features from sight till all sense of reality was lost. Fog sometimes causes gaps in sound signals, dead spots where nothing can be heard, and a ship, listening for the warning sound, can go unsuspecting to her doom. So it was this May morning, when the liner *Olympic*, proceeding cautiously but steadily on her transatlantic crossing, ran head on into the Nantucket Lightship. Her knifelike bow, in front of 47,000 tons of steel and driven by the power of 10,000 horses, cut right through the little ship. The men of the lightship had no warning; one minute they were going about their accustomed tasks, a second later ten of them were floundering in the water. The other four were killed instantly by the crushing blow of the *Olympic*'s bow. Three others died later of their injuries, making a total of seven, one-half the crew, killed in the collision. The whole story of the tragedy is still wrapped in fog; in addition to the sound of the diaphone horn, the lightship broadcast a radio beam, and she had an underwater oscillator which should have been heard on the *Olympic*'s sonar system. The captain thought the radio beam might have been inaccurate and said he hadn't received the oscillator signal at all. Whatever else went wrong that day, and regardless of whether someone was negligent or not, there is no doubt of the identity of the real culprit — it was that age-old enemy of all sailors, the fog.

After the Nantucket Lightship was sunk by the *Olympic*, light-ship engineers began to pay more attention to safety. The new vessels were made practically collision-proof, with double bottoms, watertight bulkheads, and several alternate escape hatches. In addition to the light, they were all equipped with radio beacon, diaphone horn, and oscillator for underwater signaling — just about everything needed to warn ships of danger and to guide them safely into port. They did a good job and, at one time, there were more than thirty-five of these sturdy little vessels in service. And yet, when the last of the Ambrose lightships was removed from her post in the Ambrose Channel in New York Harbor on August 23, 1967, their number had dwindled until only five were left.

Progress, economy, and efficiency, the watchwords of the times, have spelled doom for the lightship. In the war of the lights against the sea, the sea has won a battle but is losing the war; for thanks to the ingenuity of the oil industry engineers who have developed huge offshore oil drilling towers capable of supporting a great weight of housing, men, and machinery in perfect comfort and safety, most of the troubles that beset the lightship can now be avoided.

TOMORROW'S TOWERS

FOR THOUSANDS OF YEARS, ever since the Egyptians first lit their warning fires on the banks of the Nile, sailors have depended on their eyes and ears and the warning signals from lighthouses to alert them to danger and guide them safely to their destinations. The lighthouse, in turn, couldn't function without the men and women who lived in them and took care of the lights and fog horns.

Gradually, though, the picture has been changing; we depend more and more on machines to do our work and, like everything else, the lighthouse is being automated. The modern lighthouse, controlled by computer, complete with feedback systems and activated by an assortment of electronic impulses frequently originating many miles away, can get along very nicely for long periods of time without anyone there to look after it.

More and more of the existing major lighthouses — the light at Nauset Beach on Cape Cod, the towering Cape Hatteras Light in North Carolina, and the famous Tybee Light in Georgia whose beam can be seen for twenty miles — have become robot stations where the light, the horn, and the radio turn themselves on and off at the proper times. An even better example of the robot light

station is the Long Beach Light on the middle breakwater at San
Pedro, California. This white, rectangular, forty-two-foot tower on
top of a white building, supported by several short thick concrete
columns, doesn't look like the traditional lighthouse but it is
efficient and was designed to withstand all of Nature's most de-
structive attacks, including hurricanes, tidal waves, and earthquakes. And that is exactly what it has been doing ever since it
was built in 1949. In addition to the 140,000 candle power light,
it has a radio beacon and a fog horn. Originally it was powered
by four Diesel engines which, like the men they had replaced,
stood regular watches of four hours on and four hours off, with
two always in reserve. If anything went wrong it showed up on
a series of dials at the Los Angeles Light four miles away, and
someone could be sent to fix it. This was practically never neces-
sary, however, since the automatic system worked so well that
the only major change over the years has been to substitute electricity, carried by cable from the Los Angeles Lighthouse, for the
Diesel power generated on the spot.

Whatever happens in these days of electronic wizardry happens
fast, and these highly efficient semiautomatic lights are already
obsolete. One by one the lights are going out, the blaring voice
of the diaphone is getting weaker, and the radio beacon's continuous signal is slowly fading. Their places have been taken by
the pulsing, throbbing loran signal traveling for thousands of
miles through all sorts of weather with the speed of light and
constancy of a planet in orbit around the sun.

Yes, the lighthouse as we have known it has seen its day. The
beacons of the future, tomorrow's towers, couldn't wait for
tomorrow. They have already arrived and are hard at work all
along our far-flung coastline, mapping the skies with their invisible
lines of position.

The steel skeleton towers of the loran station, stabbing the skies
like giant metal spikes, are springing up on the shores of both